NUCLEAR PERIL

HARPER & ROW, PUBLISHERS

NEW YORK

Cambridge
Hagerstown
Philadelphia
San Francisco

1817

London
Mexico City
Sao Paolo
Sydney

NUCLEAR PERIL

The Politics of Proliferation

Edward J. Markey

MEMBER OF CONGRESS

with

Douglas C. Waller

BALLINGER PUBLISHING COMPANY
Cambridge, Massachusetts
A Subsidiary of Harper & Row, Publishers, Inc.

Grateful acknowledgment is made to various journals, publishers, and media for permission to reprint the following copyrighted material:

"Fuel to India," September 16, 1980 broadcast, MacNeil/Lehrer Report. Copyright 1980 by the MacNeil/Lehrer Report.

Amory B. Lovins, L. Hunter Lovins, and Leonard Ross, "Nuclear Power and Nuclear Bombs," *Foreign Affairs* (Summer 1980). Excerpted by permission of *Foreign Affairs*. Copyright 1980 by the Council on Foreign Relations, Inc.

"Pro and Con: Sell Nuclear Fuel to India?" Interviews published in *U.S. News & World Report* (August 18, 1980). Copyright 1980 by *U.S. News & World Report*.

David D. Rosenbaum, "Nuclear Terror," *International Security*, (Winter 1977). Copyright 1977 by the President and Fellows of Harvard College.

Lem Tucker's report on the CBS Evening News. Copyright 1980, CBS Inc. All rights reserved. Originally broadcast June 19, 1980 over the CBS Television Network as part of the CBS EVENING NEWS.

Steve Weisman and Herbert Krosney, *The Islamic Bomb*. Copyright 1981 by Steve Weisman and Herbert Krosney. Reprinted by permission of TIMES BOOKS, a division of Quadrangle/The New York Times Book Co., Inc.

International Standard Book Number: 0-88410-892-9

Library of Congress Catalog Card Number: 82-13854

Printed in the United States of America

Library of Congress Cataloging Data

Markey, Edward J.
    Nuclear peril, the politics of proliferation.

    Includes index.
    1. Nuclear nonproliferation. 2. Atomic weapons. 3. Atomic power
industry — United States. 4. World politics — 1945–   . I. Waller, Douglas C.
II. Title.
JX1974.73.M37 1982   327.14   82-13854
ISBN 0-88410-892-9

To my mother and father.

Contents

FOREWORD

Prevention of nuclear war is not only the great issue of our time, but the greatest issue of all time. Together, the United States and the Soviet Union possess the equivalent of one million Hiroshima bombs – or four tons of TNT for every man, woman, and child living on this planet. In addition to the superpowers, four other nations have already joined the nuclear club – Great Britain in 1952, France in 1960, China in 1964, and India in 1974. More than two dozen other nations are thought to be at or near the threshold of nuclear capability. The specter that Libya or Iraq may soon possess the bomb haunts the search for peace in the Middle East.

Nuclear weapons in the arsenals of unstable Third World regimes are a clear and present danger to all humanity. Concern for global survival will not prevail in the irrational calculations of terrorist groups. Dictators threatened with attack along their borders or revolutions from within may not pause before pressing the button. The scenarios are terrifying. Suppose Libya, determined to acquire nuclear weapons, receives a gift of the bomb from Pakistan as an act of Islamic solidarity. Colonel Quaddafi brandishes it against Israel, and the crisis escalates. The Soviet Union, Libya's ally, joins the confrontation and so does Israel's ally, the United States; the conflict quickly builds to a regional and then a global nuclear catastrophe.

As more and more nations crash the nuclear club, the risks inherent in nuclear proliferation rise geometrically; at any moment, a seemingly local crisis may suddenly escalate beyond any possibility of control. The entire earth could be in the grip, and at the mercy, of a "use it or lose it psychology" among nations with the bomb.

This book is the story of the incalculable danger of the atomic age and the insidious spread of nuclear weaponry. It is full of the experience and insight of an outstanding congressman from Massachusetts, Ed Markey, who is leading the fight in Congress for a responsible policy to control the atom. His book examines the causes of nuclear proliferation and its parasitic relationship to the arms race. And his message is compelling – the world's thermonuclear temperature is climbing dangerously, yet current policies force the fever even higher. The United States and the Soviet Union commit more time and more resources to preparing for nuclear war than to preventing it. We pursue the phantom of nuclear superiority, while the rest of the world grows increasingly apprehensive that the light at the end of the tunnel is the fireball of the final holocaust.

The Markey message drives home the utter futility of the nuclear arms race. The United States and the Soviet Union are now at approximate nuclear parity. Neither nation will ever permit the other to secure a nuclear advantage; each nation will match the other – bomb for bomb, missile for missile – on an accelerating course that may finally carry us over the nuclear cliff.

On a smaller but no less lethal scale, the same psychology is poisoning other nations. No Third World country is likely to remain idle while rivals move toward a nuclear monopoly of the region. For some ambitious leaders, the prestige of joining the nuclear club and the promise of a propaganda windfall may be enough to rationalize a fateful decision to embark on a nuclear weapons program.

There has to be a better way; slowly, but with growing intensity and influence, the American people are finding it. By the millions, from town meetings in Massachusetts to statewide ballot initiatives in California, citizens are demanding an end to the nuclear madness. They are calling for an immediate, comprehensive nuclear weapons freeze by the United States and the Soviet Union on the testing, production, and deployment of nuclear warheads, missiles, and other delivery systems, followed by major reductions in current arsenals. And they are also demanding tough measures to halt the spread of nuclear weapons to other nations.

The proponents of a nuclear freeze in America have joined citizens of other countries and continents in a worldwide grass-roots effort to stop the nuclear arms race. Political leaders still hold back, but individual citizens have already made a difference in their own lands, speaking out against an ever-escalating weapons race that threatens the survival of humanity. They understand that the earth itself is an endangered species, and that the urgent choice we face is between existence and extinction.

A nuclear weapons freeze by the United States and the Soviet Union is the critical first step to end the arms race and meet the challenge of nuclear proliferation. Absent a superpower freeze, the struggle to bar the door of the nuclear club against other nations will be even more difficult to win. American and Soviet appeals inevitably fall on deaf ears as the nuclear giants multiply their megatons. A freeze can change the attitudes of other nations. When the United States and the Soviet Union end their own nuclear arms race, other nations will lose their best excuse to start down the nuclear path.

India's nuclear test in 1974 shocked the world and demonstrated to other regimes that a nuclear capability could be within reach for any nation. The United States spoke out against the Indian test, but we missed the opportunity to put in place a more effective anti-proliferation strategy. Subsequent decisions by our government to license uranium exports to India without adequate safeguards further undermined our policy. And when Pakistan began its own nuclear arms race with India, the response from the United States again was wanting. To this day, the Administration endorses U.S. aid to Pakistan without credible guarantees against the development of nuclear weapons.

The decline of nonproliferation as a goal of U.S. foreign policy was clearly demonstrated by the comment of President Reagan in the 1980 election campaign; asked if the United States should oppose nuclear proliferation, he replied: "I just don't think it's any of our business."

I count myself a leading advocate of deregulation in areas of the economy where free enterprise can work. But it makes no sense to deregulate the nuclear arms race and encourage world trade in fissionable materials. We cannot afford the risk that nuclear power plants will be diverted to nuclear bomb production. As Ed Markey states, "At the end of the Reagan path are more nuclear power plants, more nuclear bombs, and more chances of nuclear conflict."

A credible and effective U.S. strategy to prevent such nightmares depends on many steps. Nonproliferation must be an unconditional priority of U.S. foreign policy; it must never again be subordinated to private economic interests. We must strengthen existing safeguards against diverting weapons-grade material from peaceful to military use. We must prohibit the transfer of technology for reprocessing plutonium and enriching uranium. We must insist on controls over spent fuel from nuclear reactors. We must seek nuclear weapons-free zones, such as the one already in place in Latin America. We must encourage all nations to ratify the Nuclear Nonproliferation Treaty signed in 1968.

Above all, we must challenge the Soviet Union to a nuclear weapons freeze and a reduction in nuclear arsenals on both sides. With a freeze in place, an international campaign to halt proliferation can succeed. To a world increasingly alarmed by the spread of nuclear weapons, a freeze offers the symbol and the substance of hope.

Edward M. Kennedy
United States Senate

Prologue

"The Buddha is smiling," read the coded cable sent shortly after eight o'clock on the morning of May 18, 1974. It was the signal to the Indian government in New Delhi that its nuclear bomb, buried more than 300 feet in a desert near Pakistan, had been detonated. The explosion had the force of over 15,000 tons of dynamite – roughly the same as that of the Hiroshima bomb.

Indian scientists had built the device, Indian engineers had detonated it, and when its earth-shuddering blast registered on seismic indicators around the world, India, the nation born of the persuasive pacifism of Mohandas K. Gandhi, proudly embraced it as its own, blandly describing it as a "peaceful" nuclear explosion.

The international community was not thoroughly persuaded. Pakistan vowed that it would never submit to nuclear blackmail by its southern rival. Canada, furious that the Indian bomb had been made with the help of a peaceful nuclear research reactor it had supplied, cancelled all nuclear exports to India.

India's other nuclear supplier, the United States, stood silent. India had left a long trail of clues to its bomb program, but the United States, anxious to promote nuclear power worldwide, ignored them. Finally, two years after the explosion, the U.S. government conceded and roundly condemned the fact that material it had supplied to the Canadian research reactor was also used to manufacture India's bomb.

Why all this gnashing of teeth in a world by then comfortably familiar with nuclear testing? Simply because what India had so clearly demonstrated was that a nuclear bomb – a terrifying instrument of war – could be covertly manufactured beneath the veil of a peaceful civilian nuclear program. It was no small matter.

Largely as a result of India's explosion, on March 10, 1978, President Jimmy Carter signed into law the Nuclear Nonproliferation Act, which halted nuclear exports to countries unless they agreed to place all their peaceful nuclear facilities under international nonproliferation safeguards. Two years later, however, India had still not complied with the international controls and appeared to have no intention of ever complying. Thus, on May 16, 1980, the U.S. Nuclear Regulatory Commission (NRC) voted to withhold thirty-eight tons of uranium previously committed to an Indian nuclear power station at Tarapur, just north of

Bombay. However, the President, any president, has the authority to override the NRC's decision and, unless Congress decides otherwise, to allow such a shipment to proceed. That is precisely what Jimmy Carter did. Fearing the adverse impact the cutoff would have on U.S.-Indian relations, he overruled the NRC decision.

This is the story of the battle in Congress to block that shipment of uranium to India, a nation that in the past had used such fuel to fabricate a bomb. It is the story of a new American President, Ronald Reagan, who appears intent on building more nuclear power plants and stockpiling more nuclear weapons. It is the story of failure – the failure of the international community and its individual governments to interrupt even briefly the cynical, catastrophic cycle of nuclear proliferation, a process that by anyone's definition is nothing less than the mindlessly profligate breeding of instruments of mass annihilation: nuclear bombs.

When we think of nuclear bombs, we think of the United States and the Soviet Union and the arms race. It is a dangerous arms race but a race between two superpowers that for the moment have been restrained from pushing the button because they realize each has the nuclear weapons capability to wipe the other off the face of the earth. The superpowers' arms race has received much more publicity because of the unimaginable destruction that would result if the United States and the Soviet Union fired their missiles. However, the more immediate danger is horizontal nuclear proliferation, the spread of nuclear arms to other nations, such as unstable Third World countries that might not be so hesitant to use weapons of mass destruction in a regional conflict.

Six nations now have the bomb – the United States, the Soviet Union, Britain, France, China, and India. About thirty more have the technical capability to build a bomb within ten years. Pakistan, which hoodwinked a European uranium-enrichment consortium in order to obtain technical help for its bomb program, may soon be ready to detonate an atomic device. South Africa was believed to have exploded a bomb in 1979. In the 1970s, South Korea reportedly began a secret plan to develop nuclear weapons. Israel, by many intelligence estimates, already has 200 nuclear warheads secretly stockpiled and may be collaborating with South Africa and Taiwan to develop missile delivery systems. Argentina, in the wake of a war with Great Britain over the Faulkland Islands, might be able to test a nuclear explosive device by the mid-1980s. Libyan dictator Colonel Muammar Quaddafi has a bid on the world market to buy the "Moslem bomb." Had the Iranian revolution occurred several years later, the Ayatollah Khomeini would have had bomb-potential material from the four nuclear power plants under construction during the Shah's regime.

Iraq's nuclear facilities supposedly have been under the closest scrutiny the world community has available through an international inspections system. The country's nuclear program had been certified as peaceful by a U.N. agency. It turns out, however, that Iraq manipulated oil exports to blackmail European countries into supplying it with nuclear materials that it could use to build the bomb. Israel, Iraq's longtime enemy, saw through the ruse. On June 7, 1981, Israeli jets attacked the Osirak research reactor near Baghdad and leveled it. By most reliable intelligence estimates, Osirak had been secretly gearing up to build several small nuclear bombs.

Yet, in the face of these developments overseas, the current occupant of the White House has pointed U.S. nonproliferation policy in a direction that is sure to create more nuclear weapons fabricated under the guise of peaceful nuclear programs. President Reagan has announced that the Administration is lifting restrictions on the reprocessing of spent fuel from nuclear plants. The plutonium extracted from reprocessing spent fuel can be used to fabricate, relatively easily, nuclear bombs.

The green light the new Administration has given to plutonium recycling at home and abroad now leaves the United States with few arguments against other nations converting their spent fuel into bomb-grade material. Ronald Reagan will be putting the United States back into the business of proliferating nuclear weapons-related technology.

This is not a story for nuclear physicists, arms control specialists, diplomats, or statesmen. For more than a quarter of a century, those experts have simultaneously professed grave concern about nuclear proliferation and assured the international community that civilian nuclear reactors are not only inexpensive but necessary and safe sources of energy. The experts have been proven wrong. Nuclear power is neither inexpensive nor necessary, and it is inherently unsafe. What is even more significant, however, is that those same experts have consistently ignored the essential fact that peaceful, electricity-generating nuclear reactors, such as the one Canada provided India, create, extend, and ensure the realistic potential for the production of nuclear bombs.

This is a story for the outsiders who have been excluded from the debate on nuclear proliferation – the grass roots movements that have been judged less than capable of dealing with such weighty concepts. Across the country the antinuclear movement, which protests the operational dangers of civilian nuclear reactors like Three Mile Island, has become firmly established. And in the past year, another grass roots movement, which protests the stockpiling of nuclear bombs by the United States and the Soviet Union, has emerged calling for a nuclear weapons freeze. The two movements, however, have yet to join forces.

This is the story of one congressman who pried his way into the debate and came away with the conviction that the movements should merge, for the correlation is simple: the spread of nuclear power guarantees the spread of nuclear bombs. That is the ultimate problem with nuclear power. There are more than 200 nuclear reactors around the world, and each one is a potential nuclear bomb factory.

Acknowledgments

Many talented people contributed their time and energy in helping us complete this book. My special thanks go to Peter Franchot, my administrative assistant, whose enthusiasm, tenacity, patience, and hard work made this book possible.

On behalf of Douglas Waller and myself, I would like to thank the members of my Washington and Boston staffs for their support in the writing of this book. In particular, I would like to acknowledge the help of David Hoffman, Marsha Renwanz, Joe Reid, and Ellen Mundt in the initial research and the preparation of the manuscript. Jim Wooten of ABC News was one of several writers whose editorial advice proved invaluable. I also appreciate the technical expertise provided by Jacob Scherr from the Natural Resources Defense Council and Paul Leventhal, president of the Nuclear Control Institute.

A number of thoughtful readers contributed countless hours to reviewing the drafts. They included Kate Steed, Gerry Salemme, Richard Markey, John Markey, Dan Payne, Jack Walsh, Dan O'Connell, and Steve Tocco. I would also like to thank Paul Warnke, Jeremy Stone, Daniel Yergin, Steve Flanagan, and Kirk O'Donnell for their valuable criticisms of the text.

I am grateful to Patrick Hefferman, who helped edit and organize the book. I would also like to thank Michael Connolly, president, Carol Franco, editor, and Steven Cramer, project editor, of Ballinger Publishing Company for their support and editorial guidance in bringing this book to publication.

EDWARD J. MARKEY
Washington, D.C.
1982

Boston to India

1

Nuclear Safety at Home and Nuclear Weapons Abroad

I t was a warm Saturday night in May, an unusual Saturday night because I had nothing to do. Other weekends that month had been booked solid with speaking engagements. But that night, with time on my hands, I decided to drive to the news kiosk in Harvard Square and pick up a stack of papers. I am a night person. Prime time is* after 10:00 P.M. I will often buy copies of the Boston dailies and out-of-town papers and read them until two o'clock in the morning.

Flipping through the Saturday *Globe* that night at home, I ran across an article on page three that caught my attention:

NRC Against Uranium Flow to India
WASHINGTON, May 17, 1980 – In a sharp rebuff to President Jimmy Carter, the Nuclear Regulatory Commission voted unanimously yesterday to disapprove the shipment of 38 tons of enriched uranium fuel to India.[a]

In a 4-0 vote, the NRC commissioners said they could not under the law approve the exports because India has refused to sign the

[a]For complete text of the NRC order, see Appendix A.

treaty prohibiting the spread of nuclear weapons, has refused to open its nuclear facilities to international inspection and has not ruled out the possibility it will explore more nuclear weapons. It tested one weapon underground six years ago. . . .

The NRC vote means the issue moves to the White House, where Carter already has indicated he will approve the shipments by executive order. Once he does so, Congress has 60 days to approve a joint resolution against it. If it does not, the shipments may then go. . . .

Before the NRC vote yesterday, Administration sources said the White House would approve the shipments because of the situations in Iran and Afghanistan that have destabilized much of south Asia. Sources said the shipments would be approved to strengthen U.S. ties to India. . . .[1]

My two years of battling nuclear power caught up with me. The news article raised another problem with nuclear electrical generating plants. Nuclear bombs. The ultimate problem with nuclear power is nuclear bombs.

It became clear to me that the line must be drawn somewhere to stop the spread of nuclear weapons. Jimmy Carter was falling into the same trap as other U.S. presidents. He was allowing short-term international considerations to override long-term nonproliferation goals. On the one hand, he was concerned about the spread of nuclear bombs, but on the other, he was unwilling to pay the price of strained relations with India in order to begin stopping the cancer of proliferation. The President, I felt, must not be allowed to ship uranium to a country that has already spirited away nuclear material for an explosive device and would not hesitate to do so again.

Nuclear Safety at Home

Although I am now a ranking member of three energy subcommittees, I did not come to Capitol Hill in 1976 with nuclear power and nuclear proliferation as my legislative priorities. In 1976, I believed that the U.S. government needed to curb the power of the oil industry over energy policy and that it needed to come to grips with this country's intolerable dependence on imported oil. After winning seats on the Commerce Committee and Interior Committee, as well as the energy subcommittees of those two panels, I became concerned my first two years in the House with the impact of gasoline, natural gas, and home heating oil prices on my predominantly working class district, which included my home town of Malden and fourteen other suburban communities north of Boston. As for nuclear power, I suppose I was like a lot of citizens then: only leery of how safely reactors were built.

Still, no one could live in New England in those years and be indifferent to what soon became rising citizen concern over nuclear reactors, which produced more than one-third of the area's electricity. Less than fifty miles north of Boston lay a symbol of the growing national debate over nuclear power, the still-to-be-completed twin reactors at the resort town of Seabrook, New Hampshire. In 1977 and 1978, demonstrators charged state police barricades trying to break into the Seabrook construction site.

During a February 1977 inspection trip to Seabrook, which is no more than a mile from the Atlantic coast, I remember wondering what would happen if an accident occurred and they had to evacuate nearby communities. During the vacation season, there would be chaos clearing those beaches.

As part of the same congressional inspection trip, I toured the Pilgrim One reactor already operating in Plymouth, Massachusetts. The plant's nuclear engineers went out of their way to point out the backup systems to prevent an accident. Sheathed by sturdy walls of concrete and reinforced steel, the nuclear steam generation unit was a maze of pipes, tubes, pumps, and valves. The engineers emphasized that "backup systems," and "defense in depth" are the watchwords. And of course, they reminded me, the NRC could fine a utility, or even revoke its license, for safety infractions.

The skepticism in Congress, nevertheless, was growing. I, for one, felt at this point that nuclear power could probably be tolerated as an intermediate energy source, but that the country should not depend on it to solve the energy crisis. Nuclear power simply had too many unresolved questions and problems. Safety standards, for example, needed to be more stringent. Tons of nuclear waste from reactors were piling up and no one had the answer for their disposal.

In 1977, the House and Senate voted to abolish the Joint Congressional Committee on Atomic Energy, which, since the early 1950s, had served as the nuclear industry's cheerleader and benefactor. The joint committee, for example, had fostered nuclear power's growth through vast federal subsidies (later estimated to run as high as $40 billion) and through special legislation that protected electric utilities financially in case of a reactor accident. In order to loosen its pronuclear grip on Capitol Hill, the panel's jurisdiction, on the House side, was parceled out to three committees: the Interior and Commerce Committees, which police the NRC reactor licensing authority and oversee the promotion and growth of nuclear power; and the Science and Technology Committee, which has jurisdiction over purely research-and-development nuclear programs.

By 1978, nuclear power had become an important issue but one with no significant opposition leadership. As a member of the Commerce and Interior committees, I was able to be a part of the nuclear debate. When the 96th Congress was gaveled to order in January 1979, I helped lead a successful fight against establishing federal Away From Reactor (AFR) facilities. With spent fuel piling up in temporary storage pools at reactor sites, utility companies had asked Congress for a bailout by having the federal government build central warehouses, which would collect nuclear waste, away from the reactors. The AFR facilities, however, were nothing more than large central storage pools, just as temporary as the ones at the reactor sites. The utilities' AFR plan sidestepped the problem of finally disposing of the spent fuel. I felt that the federal government should not subsidize the power companies with a program that did not solve the problem of permanent disposal of nuclear waste.

There were other questions the nuclear power industry and its sponsors had left unanswered. What were the environmental risks of the Department of Energy's plan to bury radioactive wastes in salt deposits near Carlsbad, New Mexico? How accurate were the NRC's projections on the likelihood of a nuclear accident? Were plant construction costs making nuclear power too expensive a product? Could the plutonium to be produced by the Clinch River breeder reactor in Tennessee be diverted for nuclear weapons? The more the public asked, the more the government bureaucrats and utilities executives hedged and sidestepped, and the more we all became sucked into the nuclear debate. And events began to bear out the misgivings.

Early in 1979, it seemed that the nuclear industry was reeling from one blow after another. Newspapers, for example, reported safety problems at as many as five atomic power plants across the country, from the Yankee Unit in Maine to the Surry Reactors in Virginia. Investigators learned, purely by chance, that because of a computer error in the designs, pipe fittings in the five plants might be too weak to keep them from bursting during an earthquake. If the pipes broke, the reactors would lose the coolant that keeps their cores from melting down. A core meltdown could result in the release of dangerous quantities of radioactive material.

Toward the beginning of the 96th Congress, I decided to sponsor in the House the nuclear reform bill that Senator George McGovern introducted in the Senate. Titled the Nuclear Power Plant Safety Review Act, the bill proposed a strict, three-year moratorium on the NRC issuing any more licenses to build or operate new reactors. It also required Congress to undertake a long-overdue study of nuclear safety.

Though the bill allowed the NRC to issue a license if the President certified that an area would suffer brownouts or blackouts without the reactor, the Safety Review Act stood no chance in the pronuclear Congress. The three-year moratorium proposal was introduced mainly as an educational exercise for Congress—a move to spark debate over the dangers of nuclear power.

But with Three Mile Island, the moratorium proposal took on a new life. On March 28, 1979, as utility executives and NRC officials scurried about to prevent a nuclear disaster at the Middletown, Pennsylvania plant, the world learned a lesson. Nuclear reactors did not pose merely hypothetical safety problems that backup systems would catch and, in Three Mile Island's case, 1,200 alarms would give adequate warning. The Jane Fonda film, "The China Syndrome," released that same month, was not just a Hollywood fantasy. Reactors had real safety problems that could result in thousands of persons being killed or injured.

If ever there were a catalyst for legislation to halt nuclear power's expansion, Three Mile Island was it. We decided, however, to set aside the three-year moratorium bill. The strategy now was not education, but action. The best way to get a moratorium measure out of committee and before the Congress for a floor vote was to attach a moratorium amendment to an NRC funding measure. We also decided on a six-month moratorium that would apply only to those plants awaiting permission to begin construction. Perhaps no more than six projects still on the drawing boards would therefore be delayed.

Yet, even in the face of growing citizen protest over nuclear power,[b] the Moratorium Amendment faced rough sledding in the Interior Committee. We spent days buttonholing committee members, asking for their votes or proxies if they would be absent. The work paid off. On May 9, the Interior Committee, by a vote of 23 to 7, approved the moratorium. This was the first time a congressional committee had voted to halt nuclear licensing. House Speaker Thomas P. O'Neill, Jr. predicted "overwhelming support" for the amendment when it reached the House floor.[2]

Speaker O'Neill's forecast proved premature. The pronuclear lobby lost no time trying to plug up the small crack the Interior Committee vote had made. The Moratorium Amendment was roundly criticized as "an empty symbolic gesture," a sop to the "wood-burners and Granola chompers." Joseph Hendrie, then NRC chairman, accused the amend-

---

[b]Three days before the Interior Committee vote on the Moratorium Amendment, about 75,000 activists poured into the West Front of the Capitol for a day of folk-rock music and speakers opposing nuclear power.

ment of being "cynical, political garbage."[3] Building trade unions, local utilities, and business groups in my home state mobilized against me. By the time the Commerce Committee considered the amendment on June 6, even the endorsement of powerful Democratic subcommittee chairman John Dingell of Michigan did not help. The amendment lost by a vote of 24 to 18.

The amendment quickly came to a vote on the Senate side. However, the measure, sponsored by Senators Edward M. Kennedy and Gary Hart, lost by a vote of 57 to 35 in the full Senate.

Following the Senate defeat, the antinuclear movement began to rally behind the moratorium proposal in the House. Environmental groups such as the Sierra Club, which before had been reluctant to enter the fray, publicly urged caution in proceeding down the nuclear path. The National League of Women Voters endorsed a nuclear moratorium, and the United Auto Workers began to question the safety of nuclear power.

The NRC and the nuclear industry also came under fire from the Kemeny commission, a blue-ribbon panel set up to investigate Three Mile Island. Arizona Governor Bruce Babbitt, a Kemeny panel member, declared he was "personally outraged" by the NRC's "damn-the-torpedoes attitude."[4]

Meanwhile, we sent letters to college newspaper editors across the country, urging them to write editorials endorsing the amendment and asking their readers to write their congressmen. In late September, I flew to New York City to attend an antinuclear rally in Battery Park that drew more than 100,000 persons. About a dozen activists circulated through the crowd distributing flyers that read: "Singing songs in N.Y.C. will make headlines and might even worry nuclear power proponents. But it won't change the laws in Congress. Or change the Nuclear Regulatory Commission. The MARKEY AMENDMENT can." Each flyer had a detachable postcard addressed to Capitol Hill. Ralph Nader urged the throng to mail the cards to their representatives. In the next two weeks, thousands of them poured into congressional offices.

Finally, on November 29, 1979, seven months after it first came before the Interior Committee, the Moratorium Amendment reached the House floor for a vote. The House debate on the amendment was heated. Pronuclear congressmen, such as Republicans Bud Brown of Ohio and John Wydler of New York and Democrat Mike McCormack of Washington, attacked it as a dangerous and vindictive measure.

No, I did not have a "vendetta against the nuclear power industry," I argued back. Dingell, Democratic Interior Committee Chairman Morris K. Udall, and a courageous conservative Republican from Oklahoma,

Mickey Edwards, rose to defend the moratorium. In perhaps the most memorable phrase of the debate, Edwards called the Nuclear Regulatory Commission "the Chrysler of bureaucracies."

"And yet, some of you do not want to even force the NRC to back off and look at what it's doing," he said accusingly. Edwards was right. The House didn't. The final vote: 254 to 135 against the amendment.[5]

Still, it was "a good beginning," I told *The New York Times* in an interview afterwards.[6] And it was. Considering that the nuclear power lobby had a quarter-century head start on us, we had expected to be defeated (although not by that wide a margin).

The moratorium vote had become a litmus test of congressional opinion on nuclear power – an index of where individual representatives stood on the issue. A coalition of members nervous about nuclear safety remained within reach – depending on the issue. Six months later, the issue arrived. It was India.

Nuclear Weapons Abroad

Reading *The Globe* article on India, I realized that the Tarapur shipment was a politically winnable issue. The NRC's reputation as a watchdog over nuclear power was tarnished at best. But even the NRC, to the surprise of many, voted unanimously against shipping the 38 tons of enriched uranium to India. I did not think that Congress would let Carter get away with overriding the NRC and gutting our nonproliferation policy.

The Globe piece brought something else to mind. During the Moratorium Amendment debate in November, the question with nuclear power was whether it was operationally safe – i.e., whether there would be more Three Mile Islands if the country did not pause for a while and study more carefully this energy source.

I opposed nuclear power and, in the back of my mind, I feared it. I feared it for reasons other than the operational problems the plants posed. This was an unarticulated fear of nuclear power – a fear Americans have learned to live with.

I remember my father telling me that in 1956 he voted for Adlai Stevenson rather than Dwight Eisenhower because he felt Stevenson understood better the dangers of nuclear war. In the 1950s we were afraid of the bombs that killed more than 250,000 persons at Hiroshima and Nagasaki. Now, there are too few people afraid of the bombs.

It is a tragic and unfortunate signature of our time that we have grown so comfortable with such awful weaponry. Nuclear bombs have become such an irrefutable fact of our lives that we have adapted to them without calculating or considering their force. American civil-defense analysts conservatively estimate that the effect of a one-megaton atomic bomb dropped on the city of Detroit would be the immediate death of two million persons. Even in the wildest hallucinations of a maddened human brain, the picture of two million men, women, and children dying in one instantaneous burst of violence cannot be drawn. It is beyond the human imagination, kept at a distance from human consciousness by some fail-safe mechanism that psychologically translates such unspeakable terror into the more comfortable realm of the abstract. We cope with the unthinkable by not thinking about it.

Jonathan Schell observed in an article in *The New Yorker* that

> This peculiar failure of response in which hundreds of millions of people acknowledge the presence of an immediate, unremitting threat to their existence and to the existence of the world they live in but do nothing about it – a failure in which both self-interest and fellow feeling seem to have died – has itself been such a striking phenomenon that it has to be regarded as an extremely important part of the nuclear predicament.[7]

And all the while, the experts have told us the atom was safe. Atomic power is too complex a subject for the average citizen or the average congressman, so we have deferred to the scientists, who told us not to worry. Yes, the atom has its dangerous side, but, the experts have assured us, the dangers can be overcome. The public doubts about the atom have nevertheless lingered.

Although at this point I had not tied together all the problems I saw in this source of energy (from plant safety and nuclear waste to nuclear bombs), Tarapur, I felt, represented the real danger with nuclear power. The Tarapur problem transcended the problem of plant accidents like the ones at Three Mile Island or Ginna in New York. It also transcended the problem of where to bury spent fuel. The Tarapur shipment raised the question of bombs – of sending nuclear material to a country that, in the past, had used it to build a bomb. Nuclear bombs go beyond the risks of an atomic power plant spinning out of control near a population center. Bombs reach people beyond the vicinity of the plants. They reach people who live all over the world and who have no control over their destiny if the bombs fall into the wrong hands.

As I thought about these things, the more deeply concerned I became. But it was midnight and I was alone, so I grabbed the phone and called Peter Franchot, my administrative assistant in Washington.

"Did you read the story on India?" I asked anxiously.

"What story?" Franchot mumbled back, half asleep.

"The story about the NRC disapproving the shipment of uranium to India. Carter's going to approve it anyway unless Congress stops him."

"I think I read about it."

"We've got to do something about it."

"Huh?"

"This is an issue we should be on top of."

Peter was finally waking up and recovering from the shock of my calling. I rarely telephone staff members in the middle of the night. Also, on nuclear power issues, Peter had been the catalyst coming to me with ideas. A former legislative counsel with the Union of Concerned Scientists, he had signed on as my top aide only three months earlier.

"That's a foreign policy issue," Franchot reminded me. "I don't think we have any jurisdiction over it."

He was right. I had the nuclear credentials to pursue the issue, but no foreign policy track record. The uranium shipment to India would come under the jurisdiction of the House Foreign Affairs Committee.

"Well, let's take a look at this and see if there's any way we can get a handle on it," I insisted. Congressmen who roust their administrative assistants out of bed in the middle of the night aren't easily put off by jurisdictional problems. Besides, in the post-Vietnam Congress it was not unusual for members outside the foreign affairs committees of both chambers to seize a foreign policy issue. My office has always had an activist orientation. If we observe any rule, it has been not to defer unduly to those with committee jurisdiction.

The India controversy also was a natural extension of our work on the nuclear moratorium amendment, and from a tactical and political standpoint, Tarapur dovetailed the battle we had just had with·the White House over the oil import fee.

In March 1980, Carter imposed a $4.62 per barrel fee that would have hiked gasoline prices by ten cents per gallon. The President claimed the fee was a measure to conserve energy. Actually, it was nothing more than a transparent attempt to raise revenues so Carter could keep a campaign promise of a balanced budget. The week before the NRC decision on Tarapur, a federal judge in Washington had decided in our favor on a lawsuit four other congressmen and I had filed against the President to block temporarily the import fee.[c]

The import fee battle came to mind that Saturday night because it involved a coalition of more than 300 Republicans and Democrats pitted against the President. In the India battle, we now had the oppor-

---

[c]Congress later in June overrode a presidential veto and killed the oil import fee for good.

tunity to combine our coalition of 135 antinuclear congressmen from the Moratorium Amendment vote with the oil import coalition of Republicans and conservatives who would oppose the President for political or ideological reasons.

I had no political qualms about taking on a president from my own party. Besides, if I could fight a sitting president who was about to hike my constituents' gasoline bills by ten cents per gallon just to balance the budget, I surely should be able to challenge him on nuclear proliferation.

"I think the President will be beaten and should be beaten on this decision," I told Franchot.

"Okay, I'm with you," he said. "We'll start mapping out strategy next week."

2

Atoms for Peace?

W alking into the office Monday morning, I was excited because I realized that I now would be working on a major piece of the nuclear puzzle. Franchot and I decided that one of the first things we needed was an update on the current issue. We therefore brought in Jacob Scherr, an attorney with the Natural Resources Defense Council, for a class on nuclear proliferation. Donald Fortier, a staff consultant with the Foreign Affairs Committee, gave us a political briefing on the impending vote. Franchot also called Victor Gilinsky, an NRC commissioner strongly opposed to the shipment, and Jerry Oplinger, a member of the National Security Council staff, for information on the NRC vote and the upcoming White House decision.

As we researched, it became clear that Congress would be deciding more than whether or not India should receive thirty-eight tons of uranium. It would also be deciding whether to keep U.S. nonproliferation policy alive. The Tarapur vote would become the crucial test. It would tell the world whether the United States was serious about halting the spread of nuclear bombs.

Nuclear Proliferation

To understand nuclear proliferation, it is best to start with a definition of the problem. Two types of proliferation madness torment this planet. The first is the Strangelovian version of which the United States and Soviet Union are the prime practitioners. It is called vertical proliferation and is the stockpiling of nuclear warheads by the two super-powers as well as the other principal nuclear weapon states – the United Kingdom, France, and China.

The United States now has about 9,000 strategic nuclear warheads aimed at the Soviet Union, while the Russians have 7,000 aimed at us.[a] The numbers are terrifying, considering that defense experts predict that 200 warheads dropped on each side will assure mutual destruction.

The second type of madness is one the superpowers have at least made a half-hearted attempt to curb. It is called horizontal proliferation and is the spreading of nuclear weapons to nations that do not have them. Though it receives only a fraction of the publicity, horizontal proliferation represents a threat many times more dangerous than vertical proliferation. To date, six nations have exploded the nuclear bomb, but even they might soon become the mere tip of the iceberg.

Consider: In 1964, the Nuclear Materials and Equipment Corporation in Apollo, Pennsylvania reported it had lost 147 pounds of highly enriched uranium – enough to fuel four nuclear weapons. CIA agents believe that the bomb-grade uranium ended up in Israel, whose secret Dimona reactor in the Negev Desert has long been suspected of producing nuclear weapons. The question is not whether Israel has the bomb, for the CIA concluded in 1974 that it does; the question now is how many.

Consider: European countries, deeply fearful of any cutoff in oil from the Middle East, have been easily blackmailed by one of the area's major oil exporters, Iraq. In return for not curbing its exportation of oil, Iraq had received for its Osirak nuclear facility near Baghdad (1) large stockpiles of uranium from Portugal, (2) a research reactor and technical help from France, and (3) sensitive plutonium extraction equipment from Italy. In the words of Senate Minority Leader Alan Cranston, "the Iraqis are embarked on a Manhattan Project-type approach."[1]

The Israeli and Iraqi examples – like the Pakistan bomb program, the alleged South African nuclear explosion, and the Libyan bid for the bomb – are the ones that generate the publicity. But perhaps even more worrisome is the capability that other countries have of building a nuclear bomb. Not all that could would, of course. Many of these countries are long-time allies of the United States. But the capability remains.

---

[a] SALT II, which was scuttled after the Russian invasion of Afghanistan in December 1979, would have set a cap of about 10,000 strategic warheads for each side.

deral Energy Research and Development Agency came up
list of bomb-potential nations:

- Countries technically capable of detonating a nuclear device
  within less than one year to up to three years if they chose to
  do so: Argentina, Canada, West Germany, Italy, Japan,
  Spain, and Sweden.

- Countries capable of detonating a nuclear device within
  four to six years: Belgium, Brazil, Czechoslovakia, East
  Germany, South Korea, The Netherlands, Norway, Pakistan, Poland, and Switzerland.

- Countries capable of detonating a nuclear device within
  seven to ten years: Austria, Denmark, Egypt, Finland, Iran,
  Mexico, Portugal, Romania, Turkey, and Yugoslavia.[2]

By the twenty-first century, we may be asking not who has the
bomb, but who doesn't?

The problems of proliferation run wild are staggering. More countries with the bomb means more chances of someone accidentally
pushing the button, more chances of military juntas like Argentina's
using nuclear weapons in a conflict, more chances of small wars
becoming nuclear wars, more chances of anonymous nuclear attacks
(our strategic system is established for an attack from only one other
country), more chances of nuclear civil wars, and more chances of
nuclear terrorism.

The threat of nuclear terrorism has received a lot of press. Consider
this chilling scenario from an *International Security* magazine article by
David R. Rosenbaum, a former Justice Department official and Government Accounting Office consultant who has written extensively on
nuclear terrorism:

> On September 14, 1981, 100 kilograms of plutonium are highjacked
> en route from a plutonium storage area in France to a fuel fabrication
> plant in Italy. In order not to alarm the public, the French and Italian
> governments decide to keep the incident a secret while they try to
> recover the plutonium. On October 20, after more than a month of
> fruitless search, the other governments of NATO are informed of the
> theft. They agree to keep the information a secret to avoid public
> panic.
>
> On December 24, the White House and major newspapers and
> broadcasting networks receive a letter stating that the World Peace
> Brigade will explode a nuclear weapon within the next two days. No
> one has ever heard of the World Peace Brigade.

On Christmas, a nuclear explosion of approximately seven kilo-
tons explodes on the crest of the Blue Ridge Mountains sixty miles
west of Washington, D.C. The news spreads quickly around the
world. The President appears on national television and explains to
the nation that he knows about the circumstances of the blast and the
theft of the plutonium in Europe. He tries to calm the public by
explaining that no one was killed in the blast.

The next day, a new letter from the World Peace Brigade is
received at the White House. It makes the following demands. The
United States must immediately renounce all its defense and security
agreements. It must pull back all troops and equipment from overseas within six months and immediately stop all sales and shipments
of arms. The number of people in the Armed Forces must be cut to
75,000 within one year. The United States must turn over fifty billion
dollars a year to the United Nations to be used in specified Third
World countries. A list of acceptable countries is appended to the
letter. The President must pardon all black and Spanish-surnamed
prisoners in federal institutions within the next three months.

The letter says that nuclear weapons have been hidden in three of
the largest cities of the United States and will be exploded if all of the
demands are not met.

What options do the President and United States have? They
cannot threaten to retaliate if a nuclear weapon is exploded in a
United States city, because they do not know at whom to direct the
retaliation. Thus all of our investments in nuclear retaliatory forces is
of no avail. Even a crude small nuclear device need be no bigger than
an office desk. The chances of finding one that has been cleverly
hidden somewhere in a large metropolitan area are small. If one
searches a particular metropolitan area and does not find a weapon,
what can be concluded? What is more, since the World Peace Brigade
has already demonstrated that it took the plutonium and is capable of
making nuclear weapons from it, it does not actually have to make
any more weapons. No additional bombs may be hidden anywhere.
But we could never be sure.

Will we choose to evacuate our largest cities? For how long? Will
we choose to ignore the demands of the note? Once people are
informed of the contents of the note, as they will have to be since the
terrorists could release it at any time, will people still choose to live
and work in our cities?

If the demands of the note are acceded to, what will stop more
demands from being made? Won't the Government of the United
States be permanently under the demand of a small unknown group?

The writers of the note do not have to expose themselves to find
out whether their demands have been carried out. They can simply
read the newspapers.

Will democratic institutions be able to stand the strain of such a
situation? Indeed, will any present governmental institutions,
democratic or totalitarian, be able to withstand such demands?[3]

Rosenbaum's story is fiction, and many nuclear analysts – particularly those on the industry's side – scoff at the suggestion that such a thing could happen.

On April 16, 1974, however, Boston's police commissioner received a letter stating that a 500-kiloton bomb was set to explode in the city on May 4. The threat was a hoax, and the perpetrators were never caught. But the threat is not unique.

During the past decade, there have been about fifty such threats across the United States – threats considered so serious that a SWAT-styled unit, the Nuclear Emergency Search Team (NEST), has been formed in the Energy Department to cope with them. With a 1982 budget of about $16 million, NEST agents (nuclear research scientists and technicians) will fan out in a city with radiation detectors hidden in briefcases and purses so as not to panic the civilian population. In 1975, for example, the team spent three days scouring Los Angeles for a 20-kiloton atom bomb that an extortionist claimed he planted on Union Oil Company property.

Threats are easy to make. Are bombs? Could nuclear terrorists steal the material, then design and fabricate a weapon? The experts say that it is certainly difficult, but it is not impossible. Reactors are not impenetrable. Nuclear shipments have been misrouted and lost.

In 1970, the City of Orlando, Florida received a ransom note with a nuclear bomb design that Air Force armament officers pronounced workable. The extortionist turned out to be a fourteen-year-old boy.

A crude, homemade bomb made from reactor-grade plutonium might only cause an explosion equal to several hundred tons of TNT, but such a blast would still be ten times more powerful than the largest conventional bomb dropped during World War II.

The Peaceful Atom

It was not too long ago that nuclear power frightened us. Four months after the Hiroshima and Nagasaki explosions, President Harry S. Truman, British Prime Minister Clement Atlee, and Canadian Prime Minister W. L. McKenzie King agreed to keep secret all nuclear information until international controls could be established. After all, peaceful nuclear power to generate electricity was still only speculation.

In March 1946, a control system to curb nuclear power's potential for destruction and to promote its benefits was put on paper as the Acheson-Lilienthal Report, named after its principal authors, Under

Secretary of State Dean Acheson and Tennessee Valley Authority Chairman David Lilienthal. Acheson and Lilienthal had little faith in an international inspections system ever containing nuclear proliferation. Their report stated: "We have concluded unanimously that there is no prospect of security against atomic warfare in a system of international agreements to outlaw such weapons controlled *only* by a system which relies on inspection and similar police-like methods."[4] Acheson and Lilienthal therefore advocated what amounted to a tightly controlled nuclear monopoly. An international authority would not only control nuclear activities, it would own them – from mining operations to many reactors – and would parcel out the nuclear activities to countries.

Three months later, Bernard Baruch, a U.S. representative to the United Nations, officially submitted a version of the Acheson-Lilienthal proposal to the U.N. Atomic Energy Commission. The Baruch plan proposed that once an international authority was set up to control nuclear resources and facilities, all nuclear weapons would be destroyed. (Although never stated publicly, U.S. officials hoped the plan would specifically keep nuclear technology and the bomb out of the hands of the Soviet Union.)

The Russians did not accept the plan. Repudiating the U.S. initiative, they turned the tables and proposed that all nuclear weapons be destroyed, before the control system would be installed. Thus, the Baruch Plan floundered for two years, and, in 1949, Russia exploded a nuclear device. Three years later, Great Britain set off a nuclear bomb and soon thereafter announced it would build a nuclear power plant. Several other countries, including India, said they would also build nuclear power stations.

So, with Moscow already knowing the secret of the bomb, and the U.S. nuclear lobby pressing for more freedom to peddle nuclear technology, President Dwight Eisenhower decided to educate the public about nuclear power with "Operation Candor." By December 1953, he opened up the nuclear store, launching the "Atoms for Peace" program. Actually, he did more than that. He shoved the merchandise out to the curb and hawked it.

U.S. Atomic Energy Commission documents on nuclear technology were declassified by the truckload. Enough information was made public that by the 1970s it had become almost a fad for civilians to publish their own designs for inexpensive nuclear bombs. The most notable self-styled bomb designer was John Aristotle Phillips, a Princeton University student who designed a bomb that would cost about $2,000 and could be hidden in a trailer. Phillips turned down requests from France and Pakistan for copies of his plans.

Nuclear training programs flourished. More than 4,000 foreign students have been trained in nuclear physics in the United States since 1955. It has been estimated that half the "key scientists" in the India bomb program received some training in the United States.

And, in a fit of hallucination, U.S. government officials, ignoring the colossal health and engineering problems of such an undertaking, even promoted the idea of "peaceful nuclear explosions" that would move the earth for big construction projects.

The United States soon became the world's principal nuclear merchant. While Atoms for Peace propaganda calmed ban-the-bomb jitters on the domestic front, nuclear power turned out to be an important diplomatic tool overseas, especially during the Cold War. By 1955, the United States had signed twenty-two "agreements for cooperation" with foreign countries – agreements to supply those countries with nuclear materials and technology.

Atoms for Peace did not come without some controls. The Eisenhower Administration asked that an international agency be set up both to promote nuclear power and to make sure that nuclear material was not diverted from civilian reactors to fabricate nuclear bombs. The United Nations obliged and in 1957 created the International Atomic Energy Agency (IAEA).

The IAEA more than fulfilled its mission of promoting nuclear power. As for the controls, the best the IAEA could come up with was a watered-down version of the international system Acheson and Lilienthal had in mind. To begin with, the IAEA's creation was not premised on the destruction of nuclear weapons, for the superpowers were allowed to keep their arsenals. The idea of an international agency owning the nuclear materials and technology was also scrapped. In its place, the IAEA set up a system of inspections and audits, minus any specified sanctions for the violators. It was generally the type of system Acheson and Lilienthal predicted would fail.

By the end of the 1960s, however, an increasing number of countries became concerned that the nuclear suppliers may have gone too far and spawned stockpiles of weapons-potential material all over the world. The United States became disillusioned with the idea of a peaceful nuclear explosion. Even the Soviets, edgy over China's 1964 entry into the nuclear club, became nonproliferation converts.

On March 5, 1970, the Treaty on the Nonproliferation of Nuclear Weapons went into effect. It had the following provisions:

- Nuclear weapons states such as the United States and the Soviet Union cannot transfer weapons or explosive nuclear devices to nonweapon states, or help them make weapons.

- Nonweapons states cannot receive nuclear weapons or manufacture them. Nonweapons states also agree to accept IAEA inspection safeguards on all their nuclear activities. (Weapons states are exempted from this last provision.)
- In return for allowing IAEA inspectors in the facilities, nonweapons states and other advanced nuclear states are assured that weapons states will share with them peaceful nuclear technology on a nondiscriminatory basis. Also, any country can back out of the treaty with three months notice.
- The weapons states, for their part, must begin to negotiate in good faith to cease the nuclear arms race and to begin the process of nuclear disarmament.

The Nonproliferation Treaty, however, has not been welcomed by all nations. Many countries have criticized the document for a variety of reasons, many of them legitimate:

- It is discriminatory. Nonweapons states have to submit to IAEA inspectors (some of whom have been suspected of being KGB or CIA agents) snooping around their facilities and prying into their industrial secrets, while weapons states do not. To dampen this criticism, the United States and Great Britain have volunteered to alow IAEA inspectors into some of their peaceful nuclear facilities.
- It is hypocritical. Third World nations, led by India, question why they should abide by the treaty's strict nonproliferation rules while the superpowers are allowed to ignore its vaguely worded disarmament clause and continue to stockpile weapons.
- It is oligopolistic. The nuclear weapons states are given carte blanche control of the nuclear market.
- It is confining. Some nonsignatories, such as Israel, are reluctant to give up the last-resort option of nuclear weapons if a regional crisis flares.

So far, one hundred and fifteen nations have signed the treaty. But forty-eight have not, which is disturbing in that some of the nonsignatories are countries such as France, China, and India, which have weapons, and Pakistan and South Africa, which do not, but seem intent on acquiring them.

And even while the treaty was being signed, developments in nuclear technology were already under way that would seriously undermine the nonproliferation regime the treaty attempted to establish. The most notable and most dangerous development was the potential commercial use of plutonium in the nuclear fuel cycle.

Plutonium Recycling

Reactor fuel is made up of uranium-235, which is easy to split, and uranium-238, which is difficult to split. When a neutron hits U-235, the uranium divides into two lighter elements and gives off two or three neutrons plus energy. Some of the neutrons split more U-235 isotopes, thus continuing the chain reaction. Other neutrons strike the U-238 isotope, which absorbs them and becomes plutonium – a nuclear explosive (like U-235) and one of the most poisonous substances in the world.[b]

The plutonium U.S. reactors produce as a by-product each year can be used as reactor fuel. By the 1960s, even though it had not worked out all the administrative and technological bugs in the light-water reactor systems, the U.S. nuclear industry began to ballyhoo, with the government's blessing, its second generation of nuclear technology – plutonium recycling.

Plutonium recycling was advertised as a so-called conservation measure. Instead of being stored away, the spent fuel from a light-water reactor could be trucked to a reprocessing plant, where a mechanical and chemical operation recovers the plutonium from the waste. That plutonium then could be used as fuel for the reactor.

Work was begun on a second generation of reactors called breeders. Breeders are reactors that produce more plutonium than they consume as fuel. In other words, more U-238 atoms are absorbing neutrons and changing into plutonium than U-235 and plutonium atoms are being split. The reactor, in this case, is breeding reactor fuel by producing a spent fuel with a high concentration of plutonium.

Breeder reactors, which are now operating on a pilot or demonstration basis in a few foreign countries, have been touted by the nuclear industry as a way to conserve uranium and to reduce nuclear waste because the breeder's spent fuel can be recycled back into the reactor. The spent fuel from the breeder is sent to the reprocessing plant, where the plutonium is extracted. In fact, the breeder reactor, because it is designed specifically to produce the extra plutonium, is committed to the reprocessing operation.

---

[b]For a brief description of the nuclear fuel cycle, see Appendix B.

But plutonium, whether it is recycled from light-water reactors or bred from breeder reactors, has one snag. It can be converted relatively easily into nuclear bombs.

No one much cared about that fact. In their headlong rush to promote the peaceful benefits of the atom, government and industry ignored – some say even covered up – the link between plutonium and the bomb.

By the mid-1970s, however, America's fascination with plutonium recycling and breeders was going through a period of disillusionment. Researchers, such as physicist Thomas Cochran and energy economist Vince Taylor, began to question the economic attractiveness of using plutonium. The argument that reprocessing and breeders would conserve dwindling uranium supplies was specious. While uranium supplies will eventually dry up, they are far from being exhausted at the moment. The fact is, the world has plenty of natural uranium, which is unusable for weapons and is more than enough to last past the year 2000.

Pioneering works by political scientist Albert Wohlstetter and the Ford Foundation's 1977 study, *Nuclear Power Issues and Choices* (administered by the MITRE Corporation), revealed the technical facade that had been conveniently erected between reprocessed plutonium and nuclear weapons.

The plutonium in spent reactor fuel is too diluted to be of much use unless it is separated from the fuel. Separating the bomb-grade plutonium from the spent fuel can be a complex undertaking, too complex and too expensive for most countries – or so it was thought. But the only other way to obtain bomb-grade material is to enrich the natural uranium to increase the concentration of U-235. Enriching uranium, however, turns out to be a much more expensive and complex process than reprocessing spent fuel. In fact, reprocessing spent fuel would not be difficult for a country and would be simple compared to enriching natural uranium, Wohlstetter reported. His study revealed that what had been advertised by the nuclear industry and government as a reprocessing barrier to keep countries away from the bomb was in fact no barrier at all.[5]

The industry and government line also had been that even if a country obtained the plutonium through reprocessing, it was too poor a grade of fuel for bombs. The reprocessed plutonium was thought to be too contaminated with isotopes like plutonium-240 and plutonium-242, which make it dangerous and difficult to handle when used for a weapon.

The Ford-MITRE report concluded, however, that these contaminants would not be a barrier to building the bomb. They might "lower the probability that less skilled terrorists would be able to make a high-yield weapon from stolen reactor plutonium. . . . But even an inexpertly assembled terrorist weapon might well have the yield equivalent to a few hundred tons of chemical high explosive."[6] A Nagasaki-equivalent bomb, with a yield of about 20,000 tons of high explosive, could be produced from just seventeen pounds of this plutonium.

Wohlstetter also revealed in 1977 that the United States had even exploded a nuclear weapon made from so-called "reactor-grade" fuel.[7] It appears that the path to bomb making was much shorter than anyone had thought, or conceded. Arms control analysts soon began to worry that a reprocessing facility in a nonweapons state would reduce significantly the time it would take the country to become a weapons state.

President Gerald Ford saw no reason to shorten the bomb-making gap. On October 28, 1976, he warned the nuclear industry that the day was fast approaching when plutonium reprocessing would be taboo.[8]

Five months later, the new occupant of the White House made the warning a prohibition. Billing it as a "major change in the United States domestic nuclear energy policies and programs" (which it certainly was), Jimmy Carter announced at a press conference that from then on the United States would defer indefinitely the commercial reprocessing and recycling of plutonium and that it would continue to embargo export of uranium enrichment and chemical reprocessing technology. Other nations would be asked to join the antiplutonium effort. The United States also would defer the date breeders would be put into commercial use.

"The United States is deeply concerned about the consequences of the uncontrolled spread of this nuclear weapon capability," Carter declared. "We can't arrest it immediately and unilaterally. We have no authority over other countries. But we believe the risks would be vastly increased by the further spread of reprocessing capabilities. . . ."[9]

Once a nonweapons state had the technical capability to reprocess its spent fuel and thereby extract the highly dangerous plutonium, it was feared that the path to bomb making would be considerably shortened and the light-water reactors would no longer be proliferation resistant. But as long as plutonium reprocessing was not introduced, light-water reactors were thought to be proliferation resistant since the plutonium in the spent fuel was in too diluted a form to be used for bombs. To soften the blow internationally of a reprocessing ban, Carter pledged that the United States would increase its capacity to supply light-water reactors overseas with low-enriched uranium.

But are these light-water reactors proliferation resistant? Can nuclear power be a peaceful technology if it only operates under certain parameters? Not every one thinks so.

Atoms for War

Amory Lovins, a physicist and consultant for the environmental organization Friends of the Earth, has long been one of the more radical thinkers in the energy debate. In 1976, for example, Lovins wrote an article in *Foreign Affairs* magazine proposing that instead of "hard" energy technologies, such as large central power stations, the world should choose less expensive "soft" technologies, such as neighborhood generating stations that operate more efficiently. Though Lovins' proposals have been criticized as wishful thinking, they have never been ignored.

In June 1980, Lovins teamed up with his wife, L. Hunter Lovins, a lawyer, and Leonard Ross, a former California Public Utility commissioner, to produce another article in *Foreign Affairs*.[c] This article states that "the nuclear proliferation problem, as posed, is insoluble."[10] But it is insoluble only because the experts have asked the wrong questions and made the wrong assumptions.

Ford and Carter considered reprocessing a complex undertaking that a nonweapons state would pursue "only at high cost, with great technical difficulty, and with a large risk of timely detection," according to the Lovins team.[11]

The fabrication of the bomb, on the other hand, is a much simpler undertaking than reprocessing. There are few barriers the United States can erect to prevent bomb making in a country once the country has reprocessed plutonium. The Ford-Carter policy, therefore, held that "reprocessing is very hard, whereas making bombs is relatively easy, so reprocessing should be inhibited."[12]

The nuclear industry attacks the antireprocessing policy at the opposite flank. Bomb making is extremely difficult, plutonium advocates insist; but reprocessing is not. A country could secretly construct a makeshift reprocessing facility in a relatively short time. Lovins noted that even Oak Ridge scientists have "developed a conceptual design for a "quick-and-dirty" reprocessing plant."[13]

The Ford-Carter ban on reprocessing, the nuclear industry thus argues, is futile because a country would have no trouble setting up its own crude reprocessing plant. Why discriminate against reprocessing? After all, it is only a minor hurdle for a country intent on making bombs. Light-water reactors minus reprocessing are no more proliferation resistant than light-water reactors with reprocessing.

---

[c] An expanded version of the article can be found in a book by Amory and Hunter Lovins, entitled *Energy/War: Breaking the Nuclear Link* (New York: Harper & Row, 1980).

Taken together, the proreprocessing and antireprocessing arguments point toward a disturbing fact: "both bomb-making *and* reprocessing are relatively easy." The industry argument, which was "meant to show there was no point discriminating against plutonium technologies showed only the wider dangers of all fission technologies."[14]

Instead of proving that nuclear plants with plutonium reprocessing are safe, the nuclear industry inadvertently demonstrated that the light-water reactors by themselves are "nearly as dangerous," Lovins wrote. Ford and Carter were on the right track prohibiting reprocessing because it is very dangerous, but they "did not go nearly far enough." What is more, new evidence suggests that the low-enriched uranium entering into a reactor and even uranium in its natural state "can be enriched to bomb-usable concentrations using low-technology centrifuges, . . . An effective centrifuge design was published 20 years ago. Better versions — much less efficient than high-technology commercial versions, but still adequate — can be, and have been made by a good machinist in a few weeks."[15]

It leads to the inescapable conclusion: All nuclear power plants are potential bomb factories. Civilian nuclear reactors "can be considered large-scale military production reactors with an electricity by-product rather than benign electricity producers with a militarily unattractive plutonium by-product."[16]

Rather than being alarmed over this fact, the United States and the world's other nuclear suppliers have become more or less resigned to the inevitability of proliferation. The French in particular have taken the most brazen view, reported Steve Weissman and Herbert Krosney in their book, *The Islamic Bomb*. According to secret French documents leaked to Weissman and Krosney during their investigation, Dr. Bertrand Goldschmidt of the French Atomic Energy commission summed up France's proliferation views at a 1973 meeting of the International Atomic Energy Committee. Weissman and Krosney wrote:

> Dr. Goldschmidt, the father of French plutonium, led the discussion. As recorded in black and white, he gave the inside view of the French nuclear establishment that proliferation could not be stopped.
> As he saw it, no nation could build a real nuclear arsenal in secret. But almost any nation could build a few bombs without anyone knowing. That, he insisted, "was practically unstoppable." So it did not make sense to become too obsessed, as the Americans were, with the clandestine building of a single bomb, since there was really no way to halt it.[17]

In the minds of the French, the Americans and the other nuclear suppliers, nuclear power is assumed to be such a vital source of energy that nuclear proliferation is considered an unavoidable by-product. That assumption, however, is incorrect.

The Nuclear Myth

A sort of mystique has enshrined nuclear power's alleged contribution to domestic and international energy supplies. The most urgent task the world faces is finding an energy source to replace oil. But nuclear power will never be a significant substitution for oil. Only one-tenth of the world's oil produces electricity, which is the only form of energy nuclear power produces. Nuclear power in the United States, for example, mainly displaces coal, of which this country has plenty.

Nuclear power's contribution to electricity production also is small. It provides no more than 12 percent of the electricity used in the United States. The percentage is not much higher for all other industrialized nations, and in developing countries, nuclear power's contribution is considerably less. The World Bank estimated that nuclear power produced only 1.7 percent of the electricity in developing countries as of 1980.[18]

Nuclear power's future contribution worldwide is diminishing. The United States nuclear industry, even by the rosiest projections, is in a deep recession that appears to have no place to go but down. Both domestic and international reactor firms are straining to maintain manufacturing operations. In 1973, the last hurrah for the domestic industry, 41 reactors were ordered from U.S. firms. Only 13 new plants were ordered from 1975 through 1978. And since December 1978, no reactors have been ordered.

Even more disturbing for U.S. companies is the fact that every reactor ordered since 1975 has either been cancelled or deferred. In March 1979, Nuexco, a California brokerage house that monitors the U.S. nuclear industry, predicted sixty-one nuclear plants would begin operation between 1979 and 1984. Six months later, Nuexco scaled the forecast down to fifty. By March 1981, it predicted only seventeen plants would come on line.[19]

Internationally, new reactor orders declined from thirty-eight units in 1974 to six in 1981. Nuclear power programs have hit hard times the last several years in countries such as Germany, Great Britain, Italy, Denmark, Norway, Australia, New Zealand, Austria, and China. In Switzerland, Belgium, and Sweden, where reactors generate more than 20 percent of the electricity, nuclear power is steadily losing ground to growing antinuclear movements. Only in a few countries, such as

France and the Soviet Union, where centralized bureaucracies and government subsidies suppress the economic disadvantages of reactors, are nuclear programs expanding. Across the board, however, free-world nuclear power forecasts in 1973 of 2,910 gigawatts capacity by the twenty-first century have been scaled down to no more than 750 gigawatts.[d]

In developing countries, where reactor salesmen have turned for rescue, the World Bank's 1979 forecast of 62.2 gigawatt generating capacity for nuclear power by 1990 was almost halved in 1980, when it forecast 38.1 gigawatt capacity for the end of the decade.[20]

A combination of factors has contributed to nuclear power's downturn. Electricity demand has slumped since the post-Arab-oil-embargo recession. In the United States, electricity demand, which had been increasing between 7 and 9 percent annually during the 1960s, has declined to a 3 percent or less rate of increase the past four years. In 1981, demand increased only a half a percent, according to the federal Energy Information Administration (EIA). What is more, the annual rate of increase for the next twenty years is forecasted at only 2.5 percent. Other industrialized nations have seen similar drops in demand. Japan's electricity demand, for example, was increasing at an average annual rate of 12.1 percent before the Arab oil embargo, reports EIA. After the embargo, demand increased only an average of 5 percent annually. But in 1980 demand was actually down 2.1 percent from 1979.[21]

As demand has dipped, the price of nuclear construction has soared. A 1,000-megawatt reactor, which cost about $350 million to build in 1971, will cost about $1.4 billion in 1988. Increasingly, financial analysts are promoting the advantages of coal-fired plants, whose construction costs are about half those of nuclear plants. "Our research indicates the nuclear power is, or will soon be, more expensive than coal-fired capacity in many sections of the country," reports the investment counselling firm Bache, Halsey, Stuart, Shields Incorporated. "As regulations have been heaped upon nuclear power, capital expenditures have skyrocketed. We anticipate that they will ultimately overwhelm the operating efficiencies of atomic units and place the U.S. nuclear industry in severe jeopardy."[22]

By the time of the Tarapur debate I was therefore convinced that nuclear power, besides being operationally unsafe and economically unjustified, also was not needed domestically. About a month earlier, as I traveled through Pennsylvania with Senator Kennedy's presidential

---

[d] One gigawatt equals one billion watts, or what could be produced by a 1,000-megawatt reactor.

campaign, I shifted from advocating a moratorium on nuclear power to proposing that nuclear plants in the United States be phased out. Oddly enough, a phaseout proposal became politically more attractive than a moratorium. A moratorium, as we discovered during the 1979 amendment fight, threatens the immediate interests of the nuclear industry. A moratorium means short-term, radical change. Construction on new reactors grinds to a halt, leaving investors with half-built facilities. Utilities are left hanging in the air awaiting licenses to operate completed plants. Thus, reactor manufacturers and construction companies react passionately to the mere mention of a moratorium.

The word "phaseout" elicits a different reaction. The nuclear lobby does not necessarily like a phaseout any more than it likes a moratorium, but it does not react to the mention of one as violently because, as a long-term change, a phaseout poses no immediate threat. The lobby also has more difficulty enlisting opposition to a phaseout, especially from utilities that have not yet made a financial commitment to new nuclear projects.

The energy loss from phasing out nuclear power could be more than compensated for by a national commitment to conservation, solar power, and limited coal conversion. A serious conservation effort could cut total energy consumption by one-third. Solar power, according to the 1979 *Energy Future: Report of the Energy Project at the Harvard Business School,* could meet at least one-fifth of U.S. energy needs by the year 2000.[23, e]

Overseas, many countries are discovering that their most valuable energy resource for the moment is not nuclear power, but conservation. For example, West Germany's percentage of energy consumption that came from oil has dropped from 55 percent in 1976 to 48 percent in 1980. In Japan, which has practically no domestic energy reserves and is strongly committed to nuclear power, a modest insulation program, recent experiments showed, could reduce heating demand by 60 percent. Even in developing countries, the World Bank reports that conservation can reduce energy demand by 15 percent in 1990.[24]

Predictably, talk of nuclear power's demise does not set well with the nuclear industry. For that matter, even President Carter's ban on reprocessing was met with indignation from nuclear proponents. "The experience of American industry abroad has convinced it that emphasis

---

[e]The Department of Energy includes in its definition of solar technologies: buildings and water heated by the sun; biomass energy from plant matter such as wood; and solar electric energy from power towers, solar cells, windmills, ocean thermal electricity, and hydroelectric dams.

on restrictive, denial type policies will almost certainly fail," complained Carl Walske, president of the Atomic Industrial Forum, a nuclear trade association.[19]

Accusing the Carter Administration of welshing on the U.S. recycling position, the domestic nuclear industry insisted that the new ban was one more crippling blow to freeze it out of the world market and allow other ambitious countries to step in. In addition, prohibiting reprocessing would not make nuclear reactors any more proliferation resistant, the proplutonium forces argued. A country determined to build a bomb would build it and no doubt leave plenty of clues for the world to uncover its intentions. Not that it makes any difference, they maintained, as there would probably be little the world could do to stop a determined effort.

But history points to different conclusions. Countries do not necessarily decide to build the bomb; they stumble into it. And India is one of the best examples of that fact.

Nuclear Politics
Carter Style

3

The Importance of the Tarapur Vote

India began an ambitious nuclear power program because of what it considers a lack of indigenous energy sources. About two-thirds of the estimated 150 million barrels of oil it consumes annually has to be imported. India's mines produce about one-hundred million tons of coal each year, but its quality is poor and the coal has to be transported over long distances to reach power plants. The country, however, has the potential to develop renewable energy resources such as solar power and conversion of waste to energy.

India decided in the 1950s to produce plutonium, not for bombs, but as part of a vague plan to develop a breeder reactor. By the early 1960s, however, India's leaders had given their Atomic Energy Commission permission just to reduce the time needed to build a nuclear device. Then a chain of events came into play to push India closer to the bomb. China, with whom India had fought briefly in 1962, exploded a bomb in 1964. In 1965, India had a war with its long-time rival, Pakistan, and felt wounded by a U.S. tilt toward the Pakistanis. India's leaders looked for a "distraction from transient economic troubles," historian Roberta Wohlstetter wrote in a 1976 essay. Said Wohlstetter,

> The basic decision to come close to making a bomb has to do with more fundamental long-term interests. The India case . . . illustrates the more important phenomenon, namely, that a government can,

without overtly proclaiming that it is going to make bombs (and while it says and possibly even means the opposite), undertake a succession of programs that progressively reduce the amount of time needed to make nuclear explosives, when and if it decided on that course. This can be done consciously or unconsciously, with a fixed purpose of actually exploding a device or deferring that decision until later. But it is more than holding out the option. It involves steady progress toward a nuclear device.[1]

By the mid-1960s, India's two suppliers, Canada and the United States, had become concerned that the gap between India and a bomb was narrowing. But the two nations took no action to maintain what gap remained, and they looked the other way when India resisted international safeguards. After all, India was supposed to serve as a model for the Atoms for Peace program by showing how nuclear power would provide cheap electricity for a developing country.

India is presently counting on the eight commercial reactors it has operating or under construction to supply about 4 percent of the country's electrical generating capacity. The eight reactors are housed in four power plant complexes across the country.

The Tarapur complex is made up of two 200-megawatt, American-supplied, light-water reactors about sixty miles north of Bombay. As part of the sales agreement with the United States, both of these reactors are under the inspections safeguards of the International Atomic Energy Agency (IAEA), the U.N. organization set up to insure that nuclear materials from civilian power plants are not diverted to make bombs.

The Rathjasthan plant near Pakistan has two 202-megawatt, heavy-water reactors, one of which is under IAEA safeguards because it was supplied by Canada. The other is not safeguarded because it is being built by India. The Tamil Nadu plant, under construction in a southern province, and the Uttar Pradesh plant, under construction in a northeast province, will each have two 220-megawatt, heavy-water reactors not under IAEA safeguards because India is building them.

In addition, India plans to build fast breeder reactors fueled by plutonium reprocessed from the spent fuel of its other reactors. It has reprocessing plants not under IAEA safeguards at Tarapur and nearby Trombay, whose facility reprocessed the spent fuel used in the 1974 explosion.

The two Tarapur reactors have become a sore spot in India's march toward atomic energy independence because they are not home built and therefore are subject to international controls. The Indians, however, bought the reactors from the General Electric Company in

1963 through a deal hard to pass up. The Tarapur facility was built with a $118 million loan from the U.S. Agency for International Development, to be repaid at a giveaway interest rate of 0.75 percent over forty years.

The United States hoped the sale would keep India friendly toward the West and that it would open up a market for the U.S. nuclear industry. The United States would then trade with nations that had not signed the Nonproliferation Treaty and thus had not accepted IAEA safeguards on all their facilities as long as the nations accepted safeguards at least on U.S.-supplied facilities.

Such an agreement was made with India. India agreed to buy all the enriched uranium for Tarapur from the United States for thirty years. Two hundred forty tons have been shipped so far. IAEA safeguards would be applied to Tarapur and all U.S.-supplied materials. India also was required under the agreement to guarantee that none of the nuclear material would be diverted to bombs and that none of Tarapur's spent fuel (currently 100 to 200 tons) would be moved or reprocessed without U.S. approval. The Indians have been willing to ship back the spent fuel, but the United States has put off accepting it, mainly because our country has no place to store it. Instead, the United States has tried to help India expand its storage facility at Tarapur to accommodate the spent fuel—all the while refusing to allow any of it to be reprocessed. The spent fuel contains enough plutonium to fashion more than forty bombs.

Even though the U.S. initial reaction was timid, the Indian explosion in 1974 gradually blew a hole in U.S.-Indian nuclear trade relations. India insisted that the blast was a peaceful nuclear explosion, no different from peaceful nuclear explosions the United States sanctioned in the 1950s and 1960s. Although U.S.-supplied heavy water was used in manufacturing the bomb, India maintained that it did not violate any agreement because the U.S. supply contract did not specifically forbid it from using the heavy water in a peaceful nuclear explosion. The State Department, however, had privately warned India long before the explosion that the United States would regard use of the U.S. heavy water for any type of bomb as a violation of the contract.

After the 1974 explosion, the United States tried to persuade India to make an unambiguous pledge not to use the Tarapur reactors for bomb making. India refused.

Public opposition to supplying Tarapur began to build. In 1976, three environmental groups intervened in an export licensing proceeding before the NRC to oppose further nuclear fuel shipments to India. As a result, the first public hearing ever held on a nuclear export was conducted in July 1976. The NRC, however, voted to issue the contested licenses, fearing that blocking the shipment would interrupt the electrical power supply from Tarapur and would damage U.S.-India relations.

Congress, however, had begun a slow burn over the India explosion. On March 10, 1978, it passed the Nuclear Nonproliferation Act. The 1978 act further attempted to tighten nonproliferation controls by making the licensing procedures for nuclear exports more stringent. While allowing the United States to remain a reliable nuclear supplier, the act committed the United States once again to encourage and help foreign countries explore alternatives to nuclear power.

The most controversial section of the act concerned IAEA safeguards. The United States could no longer export nuclear materials to a a non-nuclear weapons state unless it agreed to place *all* of its nuclear facilities under IAEA safeguards. The old agreements, which required that only the specific facilities receiving U.S. materials must be under IAEA safeguards, now had to be renegotiated to conform to the new, full-scope safeguards requirement.

Again, the nuclear industry squawked. Industry claimed that full-scope safeguards represented another slap at our trading partners, another unreasonable restriction on overseas commerce. It also came as no surprise that India, long opposed to having international inspectors on its soil, vowed never to submit to full-scope IAEA safeguards, especially at facilities it had built.

The 1978 act did leave some wiggle room for the State Department to bring India and other recalcitrant nations into line. To give the department time to make the arrangements, the act allowed an 18-month grace period, during which applications filed for nuclear exports could be accepted even though the receiving country had not yet adopted full-scope safeguards. After September 10, 1979, the full-scope requirement would apply to export license applications that were filed. The act also allowed an additional six-month grace period (until March 10, 1980) for nuclear shipments. A license could not be approved for a country not accepting full-scope safeguards if the shipment would be made after March 10, 1980.

The act authorized the NRC to approve or disapprove an export license based on whether the country met, among other things, the full-scope requirement. The president, however, can override an NRC decision of disapproval if he decides that the disapproval would jeopardize U.S. defense and nonproliferation objectives. But before the president's override may take effect and the shipments are made, he must submit his decision to Congress, which has sixty days to approve or disapprove it. The act specifies that both the House and the Senate have to disapprove the shipment before it can be blocked. If either chamber fails to block the president, the shipment heads overseas.

The first test of the act came a month after Carter signed it into law. The NRC commissioners split 2 to 2 on whether to license a shipment of about eight tons of low-enriched uranium to India's Tarapur power plant. They passed the case to the White House.[a] Carter authorized the shipment to be made, maintaining that a denial would undermine U.S. efforts to get India to adopt full-scope safeguards.

Congress thus was given its first chance to decide if India should be allowed the fuel even though it had not accepted the safeguards. In this case, however, Congress went along with the president.

Representative Richard L. Ottinger, a New York Democrat and sub-committee chairman on the Science and Technology Committee, led the opposition to the 1978 shipment. But, by a vote of 227 to 181, the House turned down a resolution to block the sale, thus precluding any Senate vote.

The margin of defeat in the 1978 vote was noteworthy because it was small. Victory on antinuclear measures is often defined by how narrowly they are defeated. In 1978, a shift of some twenty votes would have had the House blocking the uranium sale. Just as important were the congressmen voting against the Tarapur shipment. Even though the House Foreign Affairs Committee leadership opposed Ottinger, he managed to gather a respectable showing of liberals and conservatives. For example, one congressman who stood up and spoke forcefully against the shipment during the debate was John H. Buchanan, an Alabama conservative and Republican on the Foreign Affairs Committee. The 1978 vote thus revealed that sizeable bipartisan opposition to fueling the Tarapur reactors was in place at least in the House, and that opposition might prevail if future uranium shipments to India came up for a vote.

Another Tarapur shipment, this one for about eighteen tons of enriched uranium, did come up for NRC approval on March 23, 1979. This time, the agency was at full strength and the commissioners voted 3 to 2 to allow the shipment, ruling that the export license still fell under the grace period of the 1978 act. Congress and the president, therefore, never became involved with the export license.

On May 16, 1980, however, the NRC finally decided that India, which still rejected full-scope safeguards, had been given enough leeway. Finding that it met none of the criteria of the 1978

---

[a]The tie vote occurred because the fifth seat on the commission was then vacant.

Nonproliferation Act, the commission voted 5 to 0 to disapprove the shipment of about thirty-eight tons of enriched uranium to the Tarapur Atomic Power Station.[b]

And so the stage was set for one of the most heated foreign policy debates since the Panama Canal Treaty. On the line was the 1978 Nonproliferation Act and America's resolve to halt the spread of nuclear bombs. On one side stood the NRC, firmly against shipping uranium to India. On the other side stood the State Department, rattled by the Iranian hostage crisis and the Soviet invasion of Afghanistan, in no mood to further alienate India, and therefore just as firmly in favor of the shipment. Reportedly, after much debate within the Administration, Carter was prepared to side with the State Department. He had promised Prime Minister Indira Gandhi several months before the NRC had even reached its decision that he would authorize the shipment. Now Congress, also deeply divided on Tarapur, had sixty days to approve it or overrule Jimmy Carter.

[b] According to federal regulations, any action by the NRC is determined by a "majority vote of the members present." NRC Commissioner Richard T. Kennedy was absent on May 16, when the commission voted to disapprove the uranium shipment to India. The formal vote, therefore, was 4-0 against the shipment. The NRC reported, however, that had Kennedy been present he would have voted to disapprove the shipment. So in effect, the NRC was unanimous, or 5-0, against the shipment.

4

The First Step
Wedging into the Nonproliferation Debate

Deciding to fight the Tarapur shipment was easy. Figuring out a way to get into the fight was another matter, for it was clear from the outset that we were the outsiders.

The nonproliferation issue already had established leaders on Capitol Hill. In the House, it was Jonathan Bingham, a soft-spoken Democrat from New York, who has been one of the most influential and reform-minded congressmen in that chamber. Bingham was an author of the 1978 Nuclear Nonproliferation Act, which requires countries to adopt international safeguards before they can receive nuclear material from the United States. He is also chairman of the Foreign Affairs Committee's International Economic Policy and Trade Subcommittee, which had jurisdiction over the Tarapur shipment.

In the Senate, the nonproliferation leader was John Glenn, Democrat from Ohio, a member of the two Senate committees that had jurisdiction over Tarapur (Foreign Relations and Governmental Affairs), and another author of the Nonproliferation Act.

Bingham and Glenn were the men who had unquestioned claim to the Tarapur issue. They would be the ones to whom others deferred.

And rightly so. They were the lawmakers who had invested years in the Nonproliferation Act and were understandably anxious that it be upheld.

My legislative work with domestic nuclear power plants, I felt, gave me enough background and enough identification with the nuclear issue among my colleagues to venture overseas and jump into the Tarapur controversy. Had Tarapur fallen under the jurisdiction of Commerce or Interior, I would not have hesitated for a moment. But it did not. Tarapur belonged to the Foreign Affairs Committee. I was the interloper with a thin foreign policy portfolio—the one being eyed in briefing sessions by Foreign Affairs Committee staffers, who were wary that I was grandstanding. Nothing kills a congressman's chances of joining an issue quicker than if his colleagues perceive him as overly aggressive on someone else's turf.

But as we probed for a role in the Tarapur debate, we soon discovered a vacuum no one had stepped forward to fill. No one was taking the hard line on Tarapur. In those first few days after the NRC voted overwhelmingly to disapprove the uranium shipment, no one on Capitol Hill was voicing public outrage that the president would even contemplate overruling the NRC. The Foreign Affairs Committee staff, as near as could be determined, was negotiating privately with the White House to try to reach a compromise. No one, however, had become the aggressor willing to challenge the President head-on with a floor vote.

Franchot wrote in an initial strategy memo:

> Both Bingham and Glenn are working behind the scenes and not making public statements. Their fear is that if the presidential override is not defeated by concurrent resolution of the House and Senate and if the debate is not restricted to differences over interpretation of technical language, the guts of the Nonproliferation Act could be removed. They may save the Act by supporting the President on the Tarapur shipment.
>
> We are not constrained by such logic. We are freer in the sense that our legislative careers are not invested in the Nonproliferation Act and thus we can call it like it is. If the Act is worthless, then it should be repealed; if it is worthwhile, then it should be supported.

My not being a member of the Foreign Affairs Committee, we soon decided, posed not so much an insurmountable problem as it did an obstacle that had to be overcome quickly.

Though we were not sure at the outset how we would get on board, we knew we would have to act fast. The NRC had made its decision against the shipment. All indications were that the President soon would announce he would overrule the NRC, and already editorials from the major papers were criticizing him. *The Washington Post* accused the Administration of "backpedaling in its efforts to curb nuclear proliferation."[1] "If the United States yields to India," asked *The New York Times*, "the one nation that has actually exploded a nuclear device made from civilian materials, how can it induce other nations to accept safeguards?"[2] Even *The Wall Street Journal*, no friend of the antinuclear movement, concluded that "nothing could be more destabilizing to the region than a decision to supply uranium to India without safeguards."[3]

Since Congress would soon have to decide whether to block Carter, it was only a matter of time before a congressional office took the initiative on Tarapur, and we wanted to be in the middle of the issue from start to finish. To gain entry, we decided to be the first to send a letter of protest to the White House. An unwritten rule exists that the congressional office cranking out the first letter or holding the first press conference is allowed to run with the issue first. If we had received a letter of protest from another office, we would at least have been required to coordinate our future efforts with that office. Being first with the letter would enable us to make congressional opposition known and be a more flexible and independent member of the opposition.

We also decided not to let other congressional leaders know we were sending a letter of protest to Carter. We wanted to control the letter without being in the position of having the leadership manage our work, even if the leadership did have more clout at the White House. Furthermore, we were unsure at this point whether or not the House Foreign Affairs Committee leaders even planned to oppose the shipment publicly.

We decided, however, that the letter needed other signatures besides mine, so we passed the finished draft to three congressmen who were not a part of Foreign Affairs' leadership – John Buchanan, the Alabama Republican who spoke out against the Tarapur shipment in 1978; Mickey Edwards, the Oklahoma Republican who stood by me during the nuclear moratorium amendment debate; and Thomas J. Downey, a young Democrat and defense expert from New York. They all signed on, providing the ideological and political balance of two liberal Democrats and two conservative Republicans, urging the President "to draw the line and support the NRC decision."[4]

Next, we made 435 copies of the letter, attached another "Dear Colleague"[a] letter to each, and distributed them to the other

---

[a] A "Dear Colleague" is a term used on the Hill for a letter a congressman or a senator sends to fellow members. They all begin with "Dear Colleague" and serve as a quick way for a congressional office to distribute information to other offices on legislative business.

congressional offices. Praising the NRC for a "courageous decision" (a new accolade for us), we asked fellow members to join our unholy alliance of two Republicans and two Democrats "by signing this letter to the President expressing support" for the agency.[5]

During the next three weeks, more than sixty congressmen signed. Along with liberals, we gathered a hefty showing of conservatives, such as Jack Kemp, the Republican congressman from New York who has become one of Ronald Reagan's supply-side economic advisers. Congressman Dave Stockman, now director of the Office of Management and Budget, stopped me on the elevator several days after we had distributed our Dear Colleague.

"I signed on to your letter," he said.

"Great."

"Well, it wasn't so much the persuasiveness of your letter as it was *The Wall Street Journal* editorial against the shipment," he was quick to add. Happy to have allies for any reason, I didn't care how he arrived at his decision.

On June 12, we finally hand-carried the letter to the White House. What effect it had on the Administration was difficult to determine. *The New York Times* reported on June 4 that in the face of mounting congressional opposition to the Tarapur shipment Carter was getting cold feet and a White House decision was still up in the air.[6] India did not make Carter's decision any easier. The week before, it was revealed it had agreed to buy $1.6 billion worth of weapons from the Soviet Union.

We still believed, however, that Carter had no intention of backing down. The agitation stirred up before he announced his decision helped give us a leg up on organizing for the House vote later. The letter also provided a first step toward letting everyone know we would be a leader of the vocal opposition to Tarapur.

It was obvious we would have to play a secondary role to the Foreign Affairs Committee, whose possible opposition to the shipment carried the most weight on Capitol Hill. But if we had to accept a secondary role, we decided it would be an aggressive, high-profile secondary role, which I think Bingham & Co. eventually came to appreciate. While I stirred up my band of absolutists outside on the White House lawn, the foreign affairs barons from the Hill were inside playing the compromiser role. That relationship did not gel overnight, however. The letter to the president only got us a ticket to the fight. Any congressman has a right to move into another committee's business if he can find a reason for pulling himself into the issue. But if he enters the debate, as we did with the White House letter, and does not follow up with something that lets his colleagues know he is a credible participant, he will likely be shoved aside.

We decided to begin establishing our credibility by writing an op ed column for *The Washington Post* editorial section. The op ed piece would achieve several objectives. It would enable us to articulate our opposition to Tarapur. That way, our stamp would be on the issue and our arguments would serve as a basis for opposition arguments. Most importantly, the op ed piece might convince skeptics that we were qualified to speak on Tarapur.

The Post would provide the best exposure for the column, we thought. The paper had been pounding the President editorially for several weeks but had yet to print an outside opinion on the Tarapur shipment. After two weeks of writing and rewriting, we gave them our copy and waited.

The Post does not automatically print contributions from congressmen (it had rejected a column we submitted previously on decontrol of oil prices), but this time, the paper accepted our offering and published our column on June 9.

"Six years have passed" since India exploded an atomic bomb, the column read, and the only thing the United States has to show for its negotiations to have New Delhi accept international controls is "the back of India's hand."

The State Department, it continued, insists that "we cannot afford to offend India" because of the hostage crisis in Iran and the recent Soviet invasion of Afghanistan. "A second State Department argument, used ever since the days of John Foster Dulles, is that nuclear proliferation is inevitable – that the genie is out of the bottle – and nothing the United States can do will prevent a determined country from acquiring nuclear weapons." Perhaps. But it is not too late for the United States to reverse the damage done by spreading atomic hardware around the world without adequate controls, I maintained. At Tarapur alone, the uranium the United States had supplied so far could be used to manufacture hundreds of nuclear bombs.

I went on to say that

A new, tougher policy on nonproliferation should emerge from the Administration, starting with India. Nuclear cooperation should be halted with any country that has not agreed to give up all experiments with atomic explosions. . . . If we do not strictly apply sanctions against countries such as India that have manufactured explosives from civilian activities, then we face the collapse of U.S.

nonproliferation policy. Our opposition to the spread of atomic bombs will be ignored by country after country. Nuclear threats could emanate from virtually every region of the world.[7]

The day after *The Post* column appeared, we mailed out copies of the article to 200 newspapers across the country. These mailings in past had proven to be a valuable tactic to generate editorials from hometown newspapers, which often influence a congressman's vote more than the national publications.

In the Tarapur controversy, the eventual editorial response from mailing out the column was overwhelming. Exactly how much our mailing stimulated the response is difficult to determine, but by the time Congress voted on Tarapur three months later, about 100 newspapers across the country had written editorials opposing the shipment. Some papers, such as *Newsday* in New York, also reprinted my column, and a few paraphrased portions of it for their reports.

At the time, people on the Hill and in the Executive Branch scratched their heads over the groundswell of grass roots editorial opinion on what many considered a Washington-only foreign policy debate. "How in the world did you get to Wichita to have your column printed in *The Wichita Eagle?*" Kansas Democratic Congressman Dan Glickman asked, for example, after returning from a district visit.

After the column appeared, about 20 congressmen telephoned that they were with me on this issue. Some gave me a quick pat on the back and said they liked the piece. A brief compliment is all you expect on the Hill. Conversations are always short. If he has read your article, a congressman normally does not want to consume any more time discussing it with you. We are 435 persons dashing off to our own committees and interests. We meet for five minutes at roll calls; we pass in the corridors. It is impossible to sit down with every member and talk in any detail to change his or her position. So you work through Dear Colleagues and columns in *The Post*, hope for a nod here, a short question there.

But from that moment on, I was a serious player. In addition, the column became a lightening rod for the pro-Tarapur forces. "I am . . . convinced that the sort of 'tough stand' advocated by Rep. Edward J. Markey's article . . . can only be counterproductive," Robert F. Goheen, U.S. ambassador to India, complained in a letter to *The Post*.[8]

Four days after my article was published, McGeorge Bundy, former national security aide for Presidents Kennedy and Johnson, one of the deans of the foreign policy establishment, responded with his column on the op ed page of *The Post*. "With all respect for the excellent intentions of those who are against the shipment, I submit that they are wrong on the merits," Bundy wrote. "Failure to allow these shipments will predictably serve all the forces already working against nuclear restraint in India – it will be a self-inflicted wound for the general cause of nonproliferation."

If the United States goes back on the agreement it signed with India in 1963 to supply Tarapur with uranium and to control how the uranium is used, New Delhi will think "that the United States has broken its word as part of a process of pressure to which no self-respecting nation can submit – and Indians have at least an average amount of self-respect."

The Indian government will claim that the 1963 agreement has ended and "will then feel free, as it does not today, to make any use it likes" of the 1.5 tons of bomb-grade plutonium it can get from the nuclear fuel the United States has already supplied. The Indians also might turn to the Soviet Union for nuclear fuel.[9]

In other words, he implied, the opposition to Tarapur from the outsiders gets a merit badge for effort, but it has not properly evaluated all the facts in this case. The opposition is being simplistic. I would hear that charge again and again. The Administration's position "is correct," Bundy concluded and "is not the result of any shallow desertion of nonproliferation in deference to geopolitical crisis." In other words: "If only you knew what we know, Mr. Markey, you would agree with us." Fine. On June 11, I was to be let in on what the Administration knew.

Several days earlier, Franchot had learned that Deputy Secretary of State Warren Christopher, who would later gain fame for negotiating the release of the American hostages in Iran, planned to give the Senate Foreign Relations Committee a top-secret briefing on India on June 11. Christopher was then considered the State Department spokesman on India. Senator Edmund S. Muskie, the Maine Democrat who became Secretary of State after Cyrus Vance resigned over the failed hostage rescue attempt, had been on his new job only a month.

Franchot first checked with the House Foreign Affairs Committee staff members about how to obtain an invitation to the Senate meeting. We don't know because we would never think of attending a Senate briefing in the first place, they huffed. Since protocol had never been one of our strong suits, Franchot crossed the line and telephoned the Senate Foreign Relations staff. The congressman can come if he wants to, they said, a bit taken back by this unusual request.

Walking into the ornate Foreign Relations Committee meeting room in the Senate wing of the Capitol, I thought to myself: Here I am, a congressman not even on the House Foreign Affairs Committee, sitting with the Senate Foreign Relations Committee, the pinnacle of foreign policy on the Hill, the classiest committee assignment a senator can land. And now, I am about to receive a top secret, death-unto-you-if-you-repeat-anything-you've-heard-or-seen briefing from Warren Christopher on one of the major foreign policy controversies of the past two years.

I was about to hear the inside story on why it was imperative to support the President and ship the uranium to India. Like Della Street rushing into the courtroom with the last-minute evidence for Perry Mason, Warren Christopher was about to reveal the untold story that would change my opinion.

Christopher opened a folder and began. Forty-five minutes later, I had to leave for a House vote; but I had heard enough to know that this top-secret briefing was a sham.

Christopher recited no more than what the Administration had been saying publicly. That is, the geopolitical situation in Southwest Asia was too tense to be alienating the Indians; they might go to the Soviet Union if we cut them off; they might throw the 1963 agreement out the window and begin fabricating bombs from the fuel we had already supplied.

There was no smoking gun, no hidden Soviet battalion in Pakistan, no covert operations, no secret coups d'etat in the works. Christopher's inside information was that there was no more to the Administration's position than what we had been reading in *The New York Times* and *The Washington Post* for the past month.

"So what happened?" Franchot asked as I brushed past our reception desk in the Cannon Building. I waved him into my office and closed the door.

"Have a seat," I told him. "The emperor has no clothes."

5

The Second Step
Hearings in the Senate and House

A lopsided momentum developed on the Hill against the Tarapur shipment. The Foreign Affairs Committee leadership this time was firmly opposed to Tarapur. Because of that fact and because more than sixty congressmen had signed my letter, word began circulating that the Administration would be soundly beaten in the House. The prediction, which we were enthusiastically encouraging, was probably premature. An accurate tally would have shown that a little heavy lobbying by the White House would have made the House vote close.

The Administration, however, apparently bought the momentum rumors. It decided to concentrate on the Senate, where, save for Democratic Majority Whip Alan Cranston, a long-time nonproliferation advocate, the leadership in both parties was lining up behind Jimmy Carter. Glenn and his anti-Tarapur forces were relegated at the outset to maverick status. (Remember, under the provisions of the Nonproliferation Act, Carter only needed approval from one chamber for the uranium to be sent to India.)

So, in less than a month after the NRC voted against the shipment, the spotlight turned to the Senate, whose Foreign Relations Committee and Governmental Affairs Committee on June 18 and 19 were to hold joint hearings on the President's expected override of the commissioners.[a]

What the Senate hearings needed, I decided, was a shot in the arm from the House. Someone should go to the hearing and stiffen whatever Senate resistance there was with the message: "Help is on the way. We will win with a landslide in the House, so keep up your spirits." I had Franchot make another call to Senate Foreign Relations.

"Congressman Markey wants to participate in the June 19 hearing," he told a staff member. We decided on just June 19 because that would be the day Christopher testified and we wanted to question him.

The Foreign Relations staff had been edgy about having a congressman sitting in quietly on one of its private committee briefings. It was close to being incensed that he now wanted to actually participate in a full committee hearing.

"Well, it's rarely done," an irritated staffer told Franchot. "In fact, I can never remember a congressman ever sitting in on a Foreign Relations Committee hearing."

"How can he get on?" Franchot persisted.

"I certainly can't give you permission. If you want to write Church a letter asking for permission, you can."

Franchot sat down and typed out the letter to Senator Frank Church, Democrat from Idaho, chairman of the Foreign Relations Committee.[b]

The letter avoided specifically asking Church for permission to attend the hearing. Instead, the letter stated that "because of my interest in this area" I *planned* to attend. We also decided not to call Foreign Relations for a reply; rather, I would simply show up and if Church wanted to boot me out, he would have to do it in person.

The Senate Hearing

The Foreign Relations main hearing room in the Dirksen Senate Office Building was packed with reporters, photographers, and

[a] The 1978 Nonproliferation Act states that the Senate Foreign Relations Committee and the House Foreign Affairs Committee will review a presidential decision to override the NRC, then vote whether to recommend to their respective chambers that the President's decision should be upheld or overturned. The Governmental Affairs Committee, however, was allowed to participate in the Senate's initial hearing on Tarapur because it also has jurisdiction over U.S. nonproliferation policy. In addition to being a member of Foreign Relations, Glenn, for example, was chairman of Governmental Affairs' subcommittee on nuclear proliferation and federal services.

[b] Church later lost his Senate seat in the 1980 election to Idaho Congressman Steven Symms.

network camera crews the morning of the June 19 meeting. Spectators, lined up in the corridor, had to be rotated in and out of the gallery seating.

I approached Church to let him know I was there and, as I suspected, he did not object to my attendance. The turf guarding and protocol often is staff level only. None of the senators cared one way or another that I invited myself.

The Foreign Relations staff, nevertheless, was a bit put out. Not really knowing what to do with me, they told me to take a seat at the far end of the horseshoe-shaped committee table, on the Republican side. That position turned out to be symbolically significant because it conveniently separated me from the pack of senators clustered on both sides of Church in the center.[c]

With everyone in place, Church, who had gained a reputation in the Senate as an orator and careful student of foreign policy, whacked his gavel and brought the hearing to order.

"This will not be a simple or easy decision to make," began Church, who, along with the committee's ranking Republican, Charles Percy, reportedly had already decided to support the President. "The committee will have to consider all of the interrelated dimensions of the issue, the foreign policy implications, U.S. national security interests, and the impact on U.S. nonproliferation policy."

Tarapur "cannot be totally divorced from the Afghanistan situation," Percy added in his opening comments. "We have just seen the largest arms sale in the history of the relationship between a Near Eastern country (India) and the Soviet Union. It approaches $2 billion and the parties agreed to twenty-year terms at 2.5 percent interest. It involves hundreds of tanks, MIGs, aircraft, and other equipment.

"Despite this, to the best of my knowledge, India has stood firm in its opposition to the action of the Soviet Union in Afghanistan."

It all appeared to be an introduction to the hearing's star performer, Warren Christopher, who sat at the witness table with Gerard Smith, the State Department's ambassador-at-large for nonproliferation matters.

Christopher wasted no time letting the committee know what the White House had already given to the papers for their morning editions. "I wish to inform you," he began in a precise, even voice, "that the President has decided to authorize the exports and is transmitting to the

[c]In addition to Church and Glenn, Senators Charles Percy (Republican-Illinois), Claiborne Pell (Democrat-Rhode Island), Paul Tsongas (Democrat-Massachusetts), and William Cohen (Republican-Maine) attended the hearing.

Congress today an Executive Order and a message explaining why he believes the exports should be made.[d]

While India may have put one over on the Canadians with the 1974 explosion, it so far has abided by the 1963 Tarapur agreement with the United States, Christopher maintained. Even though Mrs. Gandhi refuses to renounce peaceful nuclear "experiments" (her code word for explosions), India insists it will remain bound by the Tarapur agreement "only so long as the United States meets its supply obligations."

"A number of considerations have led the President to conclude that the exports should be approved," Christopher reported.

"First, let us look at the negative side. If we disapprove these shipments, India is very likely to consider itself free of its obligations under the 1963 agreement. In that event, India might reprocess the U.S.-origin fuel in India and use the plutonium in the Tarapur reactors. She might order the IAEA inspectors out of Tarapur and disregard the U.S. veto power under the 1963 agreement over what is done with our fuel."

Christopher next introduced the State Department's geopolitical argument. Blocking the shipment "would cast a long shadow over our overall relationship with India," he maintained. "The turmoil in Iran and the Soviet invasion of Afghanistan have heightened U.S. security concerns in South Asia and Southwest Asia. We consider it vital to bolster our relations with this region, particularly with those countries, such as India, which can promote security and stability."

Conceding that "United States-India relations have not always been smooth," Christopher insisted that the Gandhi government has warmed up recently.

"First, India has moved from an uncritical view of recent events in Afghanistan to a view strongly opposing the Soviet invasion and calling for a prompt Soviet withdrawal.

"Second, Mrs. Gandhi recently has spoken out against the critics of our Iran rescue mission." (Christopher did not mention, however, that the week before, India announced it was shipping several hundred million dollars worth of grain to Iran, thus undercutting the U.S. embargo on exports.)

India also is trying to mend its fences with Pakistan and "has signaled it wants to develop a closer relationship with the United States," he said. If the United States ships the fuel to Tarapur it will "at a minimum, have preserved India's obligations under the existing agreements for another year or two," Christopher said, insisting that the best way to get New Delhi to toe the line is to remain a reliable nuclear supplier.

"Many in India," he warned, "see it as an index of U.S. interest in maintaining good relations and an index of our recognition of the

[d]See Appendix C for a text of the President's order.

importance of constructive United States-India ties to our broader foreign policy concerns in South Asia and Southwest Asia."

To calm congressional fears that allowing the uranium to slip by this time would gut the Nonproliferation Act, Christopher hauled out a tortured legal argument that the State Department's lawyers had devised. The Nonproliferation Act will not be dismantled, he maintained, because the two shipments, contrary to the NRC decision, can be interpreted as falling within the twenty-four-month grace period. The grace period in the Nonproliferation Act states that the new full-scope safeguards requirement will apply to any export license a country files after September 10, 1979. India's two applications for the thirty-eight tons of uranium were filed before September 10, 1979.

But the full-scope requirement also applies to any application for which the first shipment occurs after March 10, 1980; therefore, according to the Nonproliferation Act, India now had to adopt full-scope safeguards before it could receive the uranium. The NRC, finding that the full-scope requirement applied to this shipment ruled that India could not receive the uranium because it had refused to accept the safeguards. The March 10, 1980, deadline is like a guillotine, the NRC ruled. After that date, nuclear shipments to countries that have not adopted full-scope safeguards are prohibited – no ifs, ands, or buts.

The State Department, however, did not interpret the March 10 deadline as hard and fast. The six-month extension of the eighteen-month grace period, it argued, was established to prevent a country from intentionally circumventing the statute. If the act did not have the six-month shipping deadline, a country could submit a stack of license applications before the September 10, 1979, filing deadline that would enable its reactor to be supplied for, say, the next ten years without the country having to adopt full-scope safeguards. The six-month shipping deadline was established only to prevent a country from intentionally frustrating the act's provisions.

India's applications for thirty-eight tons of uranium were not filed to circumvent the act, the State Department contended. Both were filed to maintain efficient operation of the plant. Also, India filed both applications expecting to receive the uranium before the March 10 deadline. The only reason the shipments did not meet the deadline, it was maintained, was because the U.S. government delayed deciding whether to allow them. If the United States had not dragged its feet, India would have its uranium during the grace period. The Tarapur shipment should therefore be considered as falling under the grace period, according to the State Department.

Approving the shipment does not set any precedent that undercuts the Nonproliferation Act, Christopher argued, since the deadline requirements for full-scope safeguards would be met under the more liberal interpretation of the grace period.

"This action should not be perceived as a weakening of U.S. pursuit of nonproliferation objectives or of our intent to carry out the mandate and initiatives of the Nuclear Nonproliferation Act," Christopher concluded. "These objectives are of paramount importance to U.S. national security and we will continue to try to achieve them in a manner that best supports U.S. interests."

"Mr. Secretary," Church began, "the reasons you give for the decision are all pertinent and plausible. But, it would seem to me that these reasons as easily could be given next year or the following year for the continued shipments to India as they can be given now."

"We are not trying to pass on future situations," Christopher responded. "I think it is only prudent to keep future issues open. Indeed, the statute itself does provide an opportunity for a presidential waiver even after the grace period. What I would be emphasizing here now is the unique situation in which we find ourselves: two applications within the grace period for fuel under a contract which the Indians regard as binding."

"Now I take it to be the Administration's position that it rejects the conclusions of the Nuclear Regulatory Commission that the President's decision is a violation of the law," Church said.

Not so, said Christopher, pointing out that the NRC attached a disclaimer to its decision stating that its rejection of the licenses should not be read as a recommendation one way or the other on the proposed exports. The agency acknowledged that the President still had the authority to overrule its decision for national security reasons.

"What the commission did was indicate that in its view of the law, the applications were not filed within the grace period," Christopher explained. "We differ on that evaluation of the law, both as to the matter of its text and its legislative history. I think the committee certainly would recognize that the power resides in the President to go ahead with the exports, subject to the statutory scheme."

Church asked, "If Congress sustains the decision which the President has taken what does that do to the credibility of our whole nonproliferation policy?"

"Mr. Chairman, that is a very pertinent and searching question," Christopher answered with a thick slice of congressional courtesy. "My view has been that, on balance, it strengthens our nonproliferation policy rather than weakens it."

Percy next questioned Christopher. "I wonder if you would comment on the arms sales from the Soviet Union to India?" he asked.

"Unquestionably, the Soviet Union is using its resources to try to build a more solid relationship with India," Christopher said, adding that the sale had been in the works for almost two years. "I regard that arms deal as a reason for approving these applications, rather than turning them down. I think it would be the height of folly for us . . . to give India an irritant in our relationship that simply would play into the hands of those who would be supporting the Soviets."

"Are you rather pleased, as I am, that despite this very large arms sale, India has stood firm in its opposition to the Soviet action in Afghanistan?" Percy asked.

"Yes," said Christopher, "I think it is a convincing indication of the depth of the concern, perhaps not all publicly expressed, by the Indians about the Afghan invasion."

Up to then, the questioning was not too harsh. Glenn, on the other hand, came out swinging.

"I do not like pretense," he said bluntly. "It seems to me that the only thing worse than not having a strong nonproliferation policy is to pretend that we have such a policy. The credibility of our government is not enhanced by statements which claim we are committed to following one policy, yet through our actions, we are proclaiming very loudly and very clearly that we are following another course.

"I can well understand the sensitivity of the Administration to charges that another flip-flop in policy is in the works."

He then began to topple Christopher's arguments. The State Department's interpretation of the grace period is legal gibberish; "the NRC has interpreted this correctly."

"So I, for one, cannot pretend that if Congress lets these fuel licenses go by . . . the law will not have been seriously undermined," Glenn said, adding, a bit irritated, "I, for one, wish that the State Department had spent as much time trying to find ways to agree with the Nuclear Nonproliferation Act as it has spent trying to say that there is no guillotine provision in the law."

State Department officials were publicly and privately acknowledging the guillotine provision as far back as two years ago, the senator pointed out. "Now it appears to be somewhat in doubt," he said.

The Administration's fear that the Indians might cancel the safeguards agreement on Tarapur and reprocess its spent fuel without U.S. permission is misguided, Glenn contended. In the next few years the Indians will have thousands of kilograms of unsafeguarded plutonium if they do not accept full-scope safeguards; Tarapur's plutonium totals no more than a few hundred kilograms.

Glenn also had a legal argument up his sleeve. The U.S.-India agreement states that this country must supply Tarapur with enough fuel for the "full loading" of the power station plus a little extra to permit its efficient and continuous operation.

"Indeed, the Indians are prohibited from having fresh fuel in excess of the amount that is needed to supply the Tarapur reactors," he said.

By the NRC's calculation (which the State Department disputed), Tarapur's reactors already had enough fuel for "efficient and continuous operation" until February 1982.

"By that time we could take vitally important steps to change the current situation," Glenn reasoned. "For example, we could negotiate an arrangement for the return of our spent fuel, or make further progress on the full-scope safeguards question. In the meantime, instead of caving in on the basic criteria in the Nonproliferation Act, we would have enforced it."

Legal jousting aside, the issue for Glenn was still bombs. "India has indicated that she is going ahead with what are now called 'nuclear experiments.' They are not called PNEs [peaceful nuclear explosions] anymore, but are called nuclear experiments. . . . It seems to me that the question is whether we are to be a party to [India's] nuclear explosions or whether we are to say that we have had enough and we really meant it when we passed the Nuclear Nonproliferation Act? Are we going to enforce the Nuclear Nonproliferation Act? If that means that the United States drops out of some contracts we might otherwise have or get, so be it. Or will we change the Nuclear Nonproliferation Act so that we can participate?"

Glenn's frustration over this dilemma began to show: "The Nuclear Nonproliferation Act apparently is either not working or is being brought to its demise here, as I see it. Other nations are not following our lead with NNPA. Perhaps it is time to reverse some of our decisions and go back to the other option, which was to get as involved as possible all over the world and hope for the best.

"Maybe that is the best way to go. I don't know. But I do know that I wish this had not been sent up here at this time."

"Senator Glenn, we know of your deep interest in nonproliferation and this act," Christopher responded. "Where I sharply differ from you, Senator Glenn, is I feel that going ahead with this unique case does not constitute any kind of precedent and does not undermine the act for which you have a large responsibility."

Senator William Cohen, Republican from Maine, was up next. "Mr. Secretary and Mr. Ambassador, my concern is that this will be perceived as the United States raising a white flag of impotence and weakness once again," he said. "Now it appears that India has us over the barrel regarding our nuclear nonproliferation policy, and we are about to be rolled over that particular barrel. . . . There is a perception that is rampant throughout the world that every time we come to a confrontational situation, the United States retreats. . . . Frankly, I think this is a continuation of that perception."

For partisan reasons, Cohen may have been overstating the case. We guessed that Tarapur would draw Republican opposition because it offered the GOP a chance to embarrass the Administration in an election year. I no doubt was suspected of the same tactic, as I supported Kennedy in the Democratic primaries.

About this time, however, I began to tune out the testimony. I had walked into the hearing room with a prepared statement in hand, but I sat down not knowing if I would be given a chance to read it. About midway through Glenn's questions, I checked with Church about obtaining five minutes to speak. "I'll take care of it," Church said.

Back at my seat, I began scribbling over the speech Franchot and I had prepared. Although there were a number of points to make, I wanted to be brief. I wanted to appear in stark contrast to Christopher. My goal was to draw the line, to serve notice that the House will demolish Carter's override.

We started whispering strategy back and forth, looking for short sentences that would frame in the minds of the listeners what was at stake with Tarapur. Above all, I did not want to be drawn into a legal debate with Christopher.

Finally, after Democrat Paul Tsongas of Massachusetts finished his questions, I was given my chance. "Congressman Markey has asked to be recognized," Church announced. "He has been patient and has waited for the Senators first to ask their questions. As a matter of courtesy, we welcome him here to the other side of the Capitol."

"Mr. Chairman, I will acquiesce to his asking the questions if he just does not get used to being a Senator," joked Tsongas, who came to the Senate from my state's congressional ranks.

"You assume that there will not be another vacancy, soon, and I have not accepted that as definitive," I kidded back, referring to the Kennedy-Carter primary battle.

"Neither have I," Tsongas smiled.

I started by informing Christopher of the resolution of disapproval I was introducing in the House that day to override the President's executive order.

"It is my personal view that the House will move quickly to block — by a wide margin — the sale of nuclear fuel to India," I predicted. "I hope the same will occur on the Senate side.

"It will be a lopsided vote against the President, which will be a serious political defeat for him with international implications for the U.S. image abroad.

"Mr. Secretary, the way I look at it . . . we no longer have a nuclear nonproliferation policy. What we have is a selective *proliferation* policy.

"What we are allowing is for Prime Minister Gandhi, by her stone-walling, to set an example to other countries in the world that if they are recalcitrant, if they refuse to abide by the restrictions which we have placed upon the Indian government, they, too, can be sure that they might also be able to dictate our nonproliferation policy.

"I think what we are witnessing here today," I said, looking squarely at Christopher, "is the collapse, the failure, of our nonproliferation policy.

"Indeed, we are sending a signal to the rest of the world of our inability to stand by the principles which we so correctly enunciated two years ago with our Nonproliferation Act. I think we would set a very poor precedent for our future negotiations with other countries which would be seeking similar kinds of nuclear shipments from the United States.

"Would you comment on that, please?"

If Christopher sweats, he sweats ice water. Not batting an eye, he coolly answered, "Congressman Markey, you and I view this matter differently. I cannot see it with the simplicity that you do."

Translated: Mister Congressman, you or anyone else who does not belong in the State Department's inner circle cannot possibly understand the nuances of this issue. It was not a bad ploy, noting my junior status by labeling my arguments simplistic. He would not say that to John Glenn – not to a former astronaut who had spent six years in the Senate.

"Now I cannot gainsay your counting of votes in the House of Representatives," he continued. "All I can say to you is that the President and his advisors feel that on balance we should go forward with these shipments because they are in the best interest of the United States."

I was not so much paying attention to Christopher's arguments as I was waiting for a break in them. I did not view this hearing as a debate, where I present my side, Christopher rebuts it, and I rebut him.

There is a philosophy I have in these situations, which former Oklahoma Senator Fred Harris used when he ran for president in 1976. During that campaign, I went to a house party for Harris in Cambridge, Massachusetts. About 100 persons, squeezed into a living room, were asking Harris questions about trucking deregulation and other local concerns, and Harris kept turning the conversation to oil decontrol and company monopolies. Finally, someone griped, "Every time we ask you a question, you go off and tell us something else."

"Well," he said, "I figure I'm only going to be with you for about an hour. You can ask me anything you want, but before I leave here, there are a certain number of things I think you should know."

There were certain points I wanted to present in my confrontation with Christopher. His response was immaterial. I would hammer away at what I thought was important.

"I feel that Congress," Christopher continued, "when it looks at this matter, when it considers the pros and cons of it, will agree that these shipments should not be denied to the Indians."

"But we do that," I interrupted, "in the face of reports from India, to which Senator Glenn referred, that Prime Minister Gandhi, in testimony before the Indian Parliament, indicated a clear intention to keep her nuclear options alive in the future.

"It is clear that we, as a country, ought to accept the fact that Mrs. Gandhi will never accept full-scope inspection of her nuclear facilities and that everything else we are talking about is just so much smoke. . . .

"This is our real test. This is the place where we have to draw the line. If we allow India to breach the policy, which we have established as our national nonproliferation policy, I think we will have made a very grave mistake."[1]

I had never met John Glenn. But after I grilled Christopher, with basically the same arguments Glenn employed . . . well, it was like two strangers who suddenly discover they're from the same home town. Up to now, Glenn was Foreign Relation's lone hardliner on Tarapur. I think he now realized that he was not isolated, that I was bringing aid and comfort from the House. As the hearing wound down, Glenn slipped over to the other end of the table where I sat.

"Is this shipment dead over in the House?" he asked. Glenn is a no-nonsense person. When he says he doesn't like pretense, as he did in his opening remarks, it is because he is not pretentious.

"It's absolutely dead, senator," I answered. "It can't go anywhere in the House."

"Well it's going to be a tough fight here," Glenn said. "This is just a ludicrous policy the Administration has brought up here."

We talked a few minutes more. The exchange not only cemented our alliance, but it made clear to all in the room that Glenn was stamping his imprimatur on my participation in Tarapur.

That afternoon, CBS news called to ask if I could be at the House recording studio in forty-five minutes for an interview on Tarapur. Glenn would speak for the Senate.

"Before he left for Europe," Walter Cronkite said that evening on the CBS Evening News, "Mr. Carter left behind the seed of another likely fight with Congress. That seed was thirty-eight tons of enriched uranium which he said today could be sold to India. But Congress stands in the way, as Lem Tucker reports."

"The Administration decision to sell nuclear fuel to India took legislators by surprise," said Tucker. "After all, just last month, the Nuclear Regulatory Commission rejected India's request, then sixty legislators jointly urged President Carter to back the decision. And several very influential senators personally pleaded with the President to at least delay the sales while the law was studied and revised. Current law bans nuclear shipments to nations which refuse international inspections and safeguards of nuclear facilities, and India is such a country."

The camera cut away to Glenn: "We do very much question whether we really have a nuclear nonproliferation policy if we're going to make this sale to India," he said. "India, who has put nothing under safeguards so far, who is not a member of the Nonproliferation Treaty, and India, who has made no bones about the fact that they're going ahead with other nuclear—as they call them now—experiments, which by any other means is an explosion. And an explosion is an explosion is an explosion."

"In the House," Tucker said, "Representative Edward Markey has already announced that he will fight the sale."

"We have the entire ideological spectrum in the House covered," I said. "And I think we're not only going to beat it, but the President's going to run into a political buzz saw when that vote comes up on the floor of the House."

"Congress now has sixty days in which to veto the sales," Tucker said. "Sources here predict that the House will almost certainly do so; Senate action is less predictable. But one senator said the damage has been done— For years the administration has been preaching nuclear nonproliferation, but hasn't been listening to its own sermons, and now the world will not let it forget it.'

"Lem Tucker, CBS News, Capitol Hill."[2]

The House Hearing

We shifted gears after June 19. No longer were we trying to jawbone Carter into supporting the NRC. Now we focused on how to beat him — and beat him badly—when the House voted on his executive order.

A week after the Senate hearing, Christopher and Ambassador Smith returned to Capitol Hill to repeat the Administration arguments before a House Foreign Affairs Committee hearing, at which I also testified.

I enjoyed the Foreign Affairs Committee hearing on June 26. This time, we were an integral part of the Tarapur debate. We had sent the letter to the President, we had written *The Washington Post* column, we had crashed the Senate hearing. And, unlike Foreign Relations, the leadership in Foreign Affairs—Committee Chairman Clemment J. Zablocki, Democrat from Wisconsin, and ranking Republican member William S. Broomfield from Michigan—opposed the Tarapur shipment. Also, the latest head count had more than twenty of the thirty-four committee members supporting Bingham's disapproval resolution.[e]

New York Republican Congressman John Wydler, a long-time nuclear proponent, was brought in as a counterbalance to my testimony. A ranking member of the Science and Technology Committee, Wydler often used his bulky frame and booming voice to intimidate nuclear critics during floor debates.[f]

But the Foreign Affairs Committee was hostile territory for him. "I am a little bit ready to plead my case before a jury . . . that has already rendered a verdict," he noted dryly at the beginning of his testimony. Still, Wydler made a stab at changing the verdict with the nuclear industry's arguments.

"If we decide not to send the fuel, we lose the market," he claimed. "The market will go somewhere else. It may go to the Soviet Union; it may not. It is likely to go to the Soviet Union, but if it does not, it is likely to go somewhere else. . . .

"The most serious flaw in the Administration's approach is it has tried to apply an inflexible, misguided policy in a unilateral fashion, with no distinction between treatment of friend or foe. As a result, all are suspected of being capable of making a political decision to manufacture nuclear weapons."

Criticizing the "Carter policy of denial" as "one of our most myopic decisions in recent years," Wydler complained that "we have alienated our friends around the world, handed power and influence to our enemies, and lost billions of dollars in sales for U.S. industry.

---

[e] I had introduced a similar disapproval resolution. But by this time, we had agreed to defer to Bingham's resolution. All the resolutions are in Appendix D.

[f] Wydler resigned from the House at the end of the 96th Congress in 1980.

"My final point is, this sale is the first time President Carter has shown flexibility on a nuclear sale. We therefore would be foolish to rebuff him on it even though this is the politically easy thing to do."

Wydler then girded himself for the assault. I testified next, repeating much of what I said during the Senate hearing. India is the crucial test, I insisted, and "other countries, including Brazil, Argentina, Pakistan, South Africa, Israel, and Iraq are watching these congressional deliberations with the closest attention. . . .

"The long-term national security interests of our nonproliferation policy must take priority over the elusive short-term goals of better relations with India envisioned by the State Department. To make an exception for India, Mr. Chairman, will effectively gut our efforts to curb the spread of nuclear weapons. Other countries in the world will realize the United States was never really serious about nonproliferation."

In light of India's refusal to accept international safeguards, "is it any wonder that Pakistan, India's neighbor to the north, complains of a double standard when the United States asks for its agreement to nonproliferation requirements."

Broomfield later picked up on my assault. "I think the larger question in this whole thing is what the gentleman, Congressman Markey, pointed out earlier about our own nonproliferation policy," he said. "In other words, what does this do as far as other countries are concerned? I am curious. How does it affect Pakistan, for example?

"I think this is a perfect example, really, of what has happened to our foreign policy. One day we have a policy, the next day we do not. . . . This is very disturbing, and I think the Indians ought to realize that we want evenhandedness. But it looks like they are bent [on having] this fuel regardless of where they have to go to get it. That is what troubles me."

Bingham went after Wydler's comment that the Russians would step in with uranium if the United States stops shipment. A tilt toward the Soviets might be a blessing in disguise. The Soviet Union, Bingham pointed out, imposes "very tight conditions on the nuclear cooperation agreements it has with India and with other countries." Unlike the United States, which has allowed spent fuel from the uranium it exports to remain in foreign countries, the Soviet Union requires that the spent fuel be shipped back, "which is probably the greatest safeguard," Bingham said. "So their safeguards policy is a tough one and not at all inconsistent, from a nonproliferation point of view, with what we are trying to do."

"Should we not be a responsible supplier, regardless of what standards other countries use?" Zablocki asked.

"Yes, that is the complaint I have heard in every country I [have] visited," Wydler answered. "The United States is an unreliable supplier."

"I said responsible," Zablocki interrupted.

"You may have contracts with us, they said, and this is not just India," continued Wydler, ignoring Zablocki's comment, "and then you come in and pass an act and impose new conditions on the contract, and now you come in after the fact and tell us we have to agree to these new conditions.

"That is not the way we like to do business, and, frankly, it is not the way I like to do business. That is what we have done in the world. We have most of the countries in this world, like Spain, who used to buy our equipment and put our plants up and buy our enriched uranium, now turning to the West Germans. . . . They will not deal with the United States anymore. Why should they? They don't want the trouble. They can get it from the West Germans and they are going to get it from the West Germans.

"We are kidding ourselves, Mr. Chairman."

Zablocki was not persuaded. "That argument could be made for the sale of very strategic and important military equipment; because they could get it elsewhere," he said. "But should we arm the world?"

"That is a different question," Wydler insisted. "That is arms. We are not talking about arms. We are talking about nuclear material."

"But the nuclear fuel we would be selling to India could end up in military use," Zablocki countered.

I jumped into the debate again. "One of the principal causes of proliferation historically," I pointed out, "has been the unfortunate temptation, which the American government has not been able to resist, to use the sale of nuclear fuel and components as a carrot to other governments for short-term transitory, bilateral interests. . . .

"Here we see a situation in which Indira Gandhi, before the Indian Parliament in March, said she would reserve the right to continue with what she would still consider to be peaceful explosions." Despite the fact that Gandhi continues to reject full-scope safeguards and engages in arms sales with the Soviets and trade relations with the Iranians, "we are willing to consider the undermining of a fundamental policy we established two years ago," to appease her.

"I would just like to point out," Wydler countered, "that we talk in this room as if Indira Gandhi is going to be running India forevermore. . . . That is a shaky government. It has changed quickly, as we know from history, and we don't know what the leadership in India might be or what their attitudes might be. So there may be some real hope we could make progress in India. I think we should keep the lines of communications open."

I was just about to attack Wydler's arguments as to the wisdom of selling nuclear materials to shaky governments, when the House buzzers sounded, signaling a roll call vote on the floor.

"The Chair will declare a recess until 11:30 and hope the members will return promptly," Zablocki ordered.

When we reassembled twenty minutes later, Zablocki invited me up to one of the committee seats so I could also question Christopher and Ambassador Smith, who pulled up to the witness table to present again the Administration's case.

"We believe the best way to encourage India to pursue policies harmonious with United States interests is to build a framework of constructive bilateral relations, which underscores United States constancy and reliability," Christopher emphasized. "The Tarapur issue is highly important in this regard."

Smith also warned that India had now put the United States on notice that if it does not ship the fuel, "India will consider itself no longer bound" by U.S. controls "but free to reprocess that spent fuel and use the plutonium as it sees fit."

"I don't know if my colleagues share it," Millicent Fenwick, the patrician Republican congresswoman from New Jersey, commented later, "but I have a curious sensation of being under the hammer."

I decided to wade in with a little crystal ball gazing. "Let's imagine now for a moment that it's 1993 and our thirty-year contract with the Indians has now expired, and all of the protections which were built into that contract theoretically have expired.

"Now, on the site of Tarapur" – which conveniently has a reprocessing plant next door – "there are now tons and tons of plutonium for which we no longer have any assurance that they will not be diverted to nonpeaceful purposes. . . .

"What statement could you make that could give this committee or the Congress confidence there will be any change in attitude now between the current commitment to the development of nuclear weapons and change of heart by the year 1993?"

"Well, I think Mr. Markey, that you are projecting a situation, which is the same as the situation that would exist if we cut off the fuel now," Smith said. "And I think that the only promise I could offer is that for some time we have at least a chance to work out arrangements for the post-1993 period, whereas if we cancel now, we don't even have time."

"You have been negotiating or renegotiating for the past two years, and there hasn't been a ray of hope you would be successful. What makes you think there is going to be any difference between now and 1993?" I asked.

"Mr. Markey, all I can offer is that history, in my experience, has been filled with surprises," Smith answered sanguinely. "And if we say we know what the situation is going to be in 1993 in India, I am not so sure of that. While there is life there is hope."

"And there is still life in the Nonproliferation Act," I fired back. "And I think the hope we have is that we are going to be able to preserve it here.

"It is a sad incident in the history of the United States and an embarrassing one," I said finally, "when the one country in the world which refuses to accept any pledge of nonproliferation of the use of these materials for nuclear bomb purposes is able to stonewall us, and we will now knuckle under to their pressure. . . . That is the ultimate weakness, the Achilles heel in your argument."[3]

The hearing soon broke up. As I gathered together my files, Smith walked to the committee table where I was sitting.

"Mr. Markey, you are a formidable debater," he smiled, shaking my hand.

"Thank you, Mr. Ambassador."

Then as an afterthought, I said quietly, "I hope you realize I respect you, but I simply disagree with your position."

"I understand."

6

The Almost Nuclear Nominating Convention

The time was ripe for a House vote on Tarapur. The committee hearings had aroused opposition to the shipment in both chambers. The House, in particular, was poised to give the President a sound thrashing, what with more than sixty congressmen already signed on against the White House and an overwhelming majority of House Foreign Affairs Committee members also firmly opposed. We needed to win by a large margin and win quickly to buck up the much softer opposition in the Senate.

But by July, Tarapur became hostage to what had been on everyone's mind since the first of the year—presidential politics.

With his Illinois primary victory in March, Jimmy Carter had all but halted Ted Kennedy's challenge for the nomination. But Kennedy hung on, and in the last ten weeks exacted a heavy toll on the President, beating him in nine key states such as New York and California. Carter, understandably, was in no mood for a House rebuff on Tarapur one month before the Democratic Convention in New York.

Over our objections, the committee votes on Tarapur, which had been scheduled for the end of July, were postponed until September—after the convention. Delaying the vote until September also put more pressure on Democrats in Congress not to challenge the President so close to election time.

The Republicans were not as charitable. Tarapur was too good an example of a Carter foreign policy flip-flop to pass up at their Detroit convention in July. Jack Kemp, one of the early signers of our White House letter, managed, over the objections of pronuclear members of the GOP platform committee, to tack a sentence onto the end of the defense plank that Republicans "oppose and deplore the pending delivery to India of nuclear material which can be directed to the manufacture of weapons."[1]

I, too, was up to my ears in presidential politics. After slogging through six states campaigning for Kennedy, I was headed for Madison Square Garden as one of his convention floor managers. But Kennedy's was not my only campaign that summer.

While I was away on a two-week vacation in early July, Franchot received a call from Doug Phelps, director of Campaign for Safe Energy (CSE), a public interest group Franchot helped found when he worked for the Union of Concerned Scientists.

Frustrated that the antinuclear movement was being walled out of the Democratic Convention to avoid embarrassment to the President, Phelps was scheming to put nuclear power before the assemblage of delegates, reporters, and cameras at New York.

"We want to run someone for vice president," Phelps told Franchot. Running for vice president is a well-worn tactic fringe groups in particular employ to obtain speaking time before a convention. Right-to-lifers, gay activists, and draft opponents, whom the Democratic platform had disenfranchised, were already gearing up petition drives to nominate vice presidential candidates at New York.

CSE, on the other hand, had become a victim of its own success with the Democratic platform. Funded by a $35,000 grant from the Massachusetts Public Interest Research Group, CSE organized in December 1979 with one goal – to make nuclear power an issue in the presidential campaign. Its game plan will probably serve as a textbook for future issue campaigns.

Twenty-five Massachusetts college students, hired on at migrant-labor wages during their three-week winter break, trudged through the snows of New Hampshire under the direction of CSE in Boston, which tracked each candidate's campaign schedule.

At every speaking stop and press conference, a CSE worker sat on the front row politely firing questions to pin down a candidate's position on nuclear power. The worker then relayed the answer to Boston headquarters, which, in turn, passed it on with the follow-up question to the CSE worker sitting at the candidate's next press conference. If candidates were forced to answer repeated questions, CSE believed, nuclear power eventually would gain the political status of, say, abortion or gun control.

The tactic soon produced notable results. Downplaying the nuclear waste program, Ronald Reagan told an audience in Keene, New Hampshire, that what the United States generated could be stored behind his podium. "If so," CSE noted in a summary of candidate positions, "Reagan's podium would have to hold 7 million cubic feet of low-level waste and over 3,000 metric tons of high-level waste."[2]

Senator Howard Baker, who fielded almost a half-dozen questions from CSE workers strategically positioned at one of his press conferences, conceded in a *New York Times* interview: "Nuclear power is becoming a major issue in New Hampshire."[3] On the Democratic side, both Kennedy and California Governor Jerry Brown early on endorsed CSE's antinuclear position.

After New Hampshire, CSE shifted resources to lobbying the Democratic platform committee into adopting three planks, which called for (1) a "national energy plan to help coordinate an early phaseout of all existing nuclear power reactors," (2) "a moratorium on all United States government licensing of nuclear power plants," and (3) a national conservation program and a shift to renewable energy resources such as solar power.

Rather than identify with one candidate, CSE began collecting names and phone numbers of Carter and Kennedy convention delegates picked after each primary. Delegates named to the platform committee were then subjected to intensive telephone lobbying, which eventually paid off.

When the platform committee convened at Washington's Mayflower Hotel in June, Carter strategists were clearly caught off balance by antinuclear sentiment in their ranks. While one Kennedy plank after another, on such traditional Democratic issues as unemployment aid, were defeated by hefty Carter majorities, here was insurrection against the Administration's more pronuclear position, and its presumed control of platform writing. But the Carter people quickly regrouped. Instead of fighting CSE by trying to whip Carter delegates into line, the White House decided to sidestep defeat and adopt the antinuclear planks; not, however, without some deft backroom maneuvering by domestic aide Stuart Eizenstat concerning language.

Instead of phasing out nuclear reactors, Eizenstat managed to have the plank the committee approved say the Democratic Party wanted to "retire nuclear plants in an orderly manner." Retiring nuclear power plants, which would happen to them anyway since reactors wear out in thirty years, was a more palatable phrase for the Administration than was phasing them out.

Also, instead of CSE's call for a general moratorium on reactor licensing until all safety problems were resolved, the final Democratic plank only said the NRC should not issue licenses until the Kemeny Commission's safety recommendations as a result of Three Mile Island were implemented. Rather than quibble over semantics, the nuances of which would probably glide past the public and press, CSE decided to accept the planks and claim victory.

CSE, however, had lobbied itself out of a job. With Carter's cooptation of its planks, CSE had no minority report, no cause to fight for on the convention floor, no roll call vote, and no friction over the issue of nuclear power that the media might pick up. Nuclear power would be buried in the stack of planks to which everyone had agreed. Even a Solar Lobby plank, which called for more federal expenditures for solar energy and which received enough platform committee support to be a minority report, was eventually accepted by the White House.

Now, two months before the convention, at least nuclear power would not spoil the Administration's plans for harmony in New York. The 3,331 delegates would not discuss solar energy, nuclear power, or proliferation. Millions of people who would be watching the convention on television would not be exposed to a debate on these issues. (The Democratic National Committee turned down CSE's written request for speaking time at the convention.) The delegates would all just have a grand old time at Yankee games and Picasso exhibits, defeating Ted Kennedy, laughing it up at the Copa and never discussing these important issues for the 1980s.

The only way to spoil the party, CSE decided, was to nominate someone for vice president, then negotiate with the Carter camp for a prime air time speech on nuclear power in return for dropping the nomination. CSE now had to find the candidate.

"We're considering asking your boss if he would like to run," Phelps told Franchot over the phone that day.

"Ed would be a terrific choice," Franchot said.

"Do you mean that?" Phelps asked.

"Sure I do."

"Would Ed be willing to risk hurting his political career to run for vice president?" Phelps said, more as a warning than a question.

Franchot returned to earth.

"I'll check."

Several days later, I telephoned the office to pick up my messages.

"Oh by the way," Franchot said, "CSE called. They want someone to run for vice president to get nuclear power before the convention. They think you would make a good candidate."

"You're kidding me," I burst out laughing.

When I didn't hear Franchot laughing on the other end of the line, I realized this wasn't a fantasy flight. Franchot briefly explained the strategy. Running for vice president is a common ploy. Julian Bond did it in 1968 during the Chicago convention.

"All we need is 10 percent of the delegates, about three hundred, and we can put your name in nomination," Franchot said.

He made it sound so simple that I knew he didn't know what he was talking about. Still, the idea intrigued me, so I didn't say no on the phone.

Back at the office, however, it did not take me long to realize Phelps was right: this would be a high-stakes exercise. My staff was divided among those who favored the candidacy, those who were skeptical of it, and those who vehemently opposed it.

I decided to bounce the idea off ten political experts across the country, people like John Martilla, who was Mo Udall's national campaign director during the 1976 race, and Jack Walsh, former Senator Birch Bayh's national campaign manager. Five said to do it. Five said don't, mainly because they did not think we could pull it off.

"It's grandstanding and people are getting tired of those sort of stunts," said Hal Bruno, ABC News' director of political coverage. Bruno called back an hour later, however, saying, "Look, I don't want to discourage you. And, as a matter of fact, if you do go forward with this, keep me up to date. It does have a certain newsworthiness to it."

I had Franchot summarize the pluses and minuses:

MEMORANDUM
TO: EJM
FM: PETER
SUBJ: NOMINATION FOR VICE PRESIDENT
The question is whether to give the "green light" to the Campaign for
Safe Energy to place your name in nomination for Vice President of
the United States on the last day of the Democratic Convention. The
clear purpose of such an effort would be to communicate directly
with the American public on the crucial issue of safe
energy – conservation, solar energy, and clean coal as opposed to
nuclear power and synthetic fuels. A second purpose would be to
appeal to the Democratic Party, both Carter delegates and Kennedy
delegates to rally behind a banner for the 80's that calls for safe
energy to fuel a new America.

You would be nominated by 300 delegates from the floor.

The message would be something like this:

"I stand before you today as a representative of tens of millions of Americans who believe in a new energy future based on conservation, solar power, and clean coal. The issue is not Ed Markey for VP. The issue is the Carter and Kennedy delegates who are here at the convention working together to get the Democratic Party to go on the record for a new energy strategy—one that says nuclear power is an idea whose time has passed, etc."

THE DOWNSIDE:

There is a risk that if the effort is done poorly you will be perceived as an opportunist. Even if it is done correctly, the leadership of the Democratic Party could be terrifically angered. In short, this is a serious decision that could affect your political career. Credibility, the loss of it, is the concern.

THE UPSIDE:

The safe energy issue is important enough to warrant an effort like this one. With a good speech EJM could push the issue.

Ultimately, the decision is yours. You can choose to proceed. There will be great skepticism, even sarcasm. You will need political courage. But the issue deserves it.

I decided to go forward with it—tentatively. With our tacit approval, CSE started putting together a game plan to have me nominated. For insurance, however, we sent two persons from my campaign staff to monitor CSE's organizing. We also recruited two attorneys from Ralph Nader's Congress Watch—Howard Symons, who handled the legal work for the petition drive, and Harvey Rosenfield, who served as our air-time negotiator in New York. We decided to have outsiders do the bargaining. That way, the issue would remain primary and politics secondary. We also wanted outsiders we trusted sitting at the negotiating table.

Up until a week before the Democratic Convention, my staff, Franchot included, had misgivings about CSE being the organization that would carry me to the podium. CSE was the typical shoestring, public interest operation—long on enthusiasm but short on sophistication. While demonstrating, in New Hampshire and at the platform committee hearings, that it could launch a successful campaign, CSE was, to put it mildly, a diverse group, from the clean-cut element that raised questions at press conferences, to the wild faction that towed a thirty-five-foot radioactive peanut down Pennsylvania Avenue with Jimmy Carter's picture on the front and Superman collapsing over it because of the peanut's krypton rays. Creative marketing, but it doesn't play well to the delegate from Dubuque.

The Friday before the convention, we sat in on CSE's initial strategy session held at the Union Theological Seminary in downtown Manhattan. What we found was impressive.

Crowded into a steamy hot classroom were more than ninety persons, all young but fairly well informed on the issue, and all wanting to do nothing more than buttonhole convention delegates.

Indeed, for a low-paid, seat-of-the-pants group, CSE turned out a finely tuned New York operation, which was headquartered in a crowded but amazingly well-organized room on the seventh floor of the Statler-Hilton across the street from Madison Square Garden. Surrounded by neat rows of phone banks and press boxes and walls covered with assignment charts and delegate lists, Phelps and his CSE lieutenants directed about six task forces to work the states. Each task force consisted of a CSE team leader, several students, a representative from the Solar Lobby (which had joined the CSE effort), and a Markey representative.[a]

On Sunday, August 10, as delegates caucused and Carter operatives braced themselves for a rules fight, CSE teams fanned out to gather signatures. The plan was simple. We would find enough delegates to sign the petition so I could be nominated, then use the list to negotiate prime time with Carter's people. In exchange for ten minutes on the air Wednesday night, in a nonconfrontational setting, we would drop the nomination. The Carter folks, above all, needed a quiet convention; it was not in their game plan to have Walter Mondale on Thursday, the last day of the convention, when the Democratic Party was supposed to be a tableau of unity, embarrassed by a vice presidential challenge.

We hoped never to have to make that challenge because, for one thing, I was not old enough to run for vice president. The Constitution states that a candidate must be at least thirty-five years old and I was only thirty-four. For another thing, I did not relish the idea of being recorded in convention history as "the maverick who ran for vice president on the antinuclear issue." For that reason, I carefully crafted a response to the countless reporters who asked why in the world I was running for vice president.

"No, I am not running for vice president," I would answer. "There is a group, the Campaign for Safe Energy, that wants to nominate nuclear power as an issue, which is at least equal in prominence to the nomination for vice president. The members of Campaign for Safe Energy

---

[a] CSE also retained, to our considerable unease, what might be called a publicity stunt task force, which, for example, put a volunteer clad in a gorilla suit and Ronald Reagan mask in front of Madison Square Garden passing out yellow solar power buttons.

believe they are getting short shrift at the Democratic Convention. They asked me if I would go up and be the spokesman for the issue of nuclear power and the role it plays in American society, if they could get enough signatures. What I am doing is seconding the nomination of nuclear power as an issue, which is one of the most important issues in America."

By Sunday night, however, our simple plan quickly fell victim to Murphy's law. In past conventions, vice presidential nominations came fairly easily. All a candidate needed was fifty delegates' signatures. This convention, the Carter people, not wanting to make it so simple for dissident groups to gain podium time, pushed through a rule that at least 10 percent of the delegates, or 333, must sign a candidate's petition before he or she could be nominated for vice president.

Three hundred and thirty-three signatures can be a lot of signatures. CSE teams had to walk from hotel to hotel, room to room, or park themselves at entrances of Madison Square Garden, scanning the crowds for persons with the right colored convention badges. Delegates then had to be pulled off to a corner for a five minute class on the dangers of nuclear power and the benefits of conservation and solar power, then pleaded with to join the petition. It was a tedious process, made more difficult, we discovered Sunday night, by the fact that few would sign on.

We knew it would be slim pickings among the Carter delegates. The President's convention managers from the start had declared our petition off limits. That left the 1,226 Kennedy delegates. But even they had been warned off our petition.

On Sunday and Monday, the Kennedy high command was pre-occupied with one thing – rule F(3)(c). This rule, which the Carter forces proposed, would bind all delegates to vote on the first ballot for the candidate they were chosen to represent from the state primaries and caucuses, thereby assuring Carter a victory. The President had beaten Kennedy in the primaries fair and square, the White House argued, so Kennedy should not be allowed to change the rules of the game at the eleventh hour. For Kennedy, defeating rule F(3)(c) and adopting a minority report that would throw the convention open was crucial for his campaign. As the later primaries had shown, political conditions had changed and Carter's support was soft and likely to fade as Ronald Reagan's campaign gained steam; only Kennedy, his supporters argued, could save the Democrats.

Both sides lobbied furiously Sunday over the open convention vote, scheduled for Monday afternoon. Carter and his wife, Rosalynn, stroked wavering delegates by phone from Camp David while cabinet members and Carter relatives hit the caucuses at the Garden. Publicizing that they were within fifty votes of catching the President, Kennedy operatives (myself included) scrambled through key state delegations, such as Illinois, New York, and California, in search of defectors.

The CSE petition to have Congressman Ed Markey run for vice president understandably was not a pressing concern for Kennedy aides.

Also, from a procedural standpoint, having their delegates sign CSE's petition might have been seen as an admission of defeat by the Kennedy forces – an admission they weren't ready to make Sunday night. Under convention rules, a delegate may sign only one petition for vice president. In the event that Kennedy won the open convention fight and wrested the nomination from Carter, he might need those petition signatures to have his vice presidential candidate nominated. Allowing Kennedy delegates to sign the CSE petition might signal that Kennedy knew he would lose before the open convention vote Monday.

Everyone who counseled us on this gambit advised us to have our delegates signed on by Sunday if we didn't want the Carter people to eat us alive. Above all, they warned, do not walk into the convention negotiating for prime time if you could not back up your vice presidential threat. But by Sunday night, we were stalled. CSE had collected less than 100 signatures – hard-won signatures from a smattering of uncommitteds or Carter and Kennedy delegates we talked into defying their whips.

Hoping to break the deadlock, Franchot, Rosenfield, and I finally tracked down Carl Wagner, one of Kennedy's two top campaign organizers, in the senator's communications trailer outside Madison Square Garden. Wagner, however, was preoccupied with frantically trying to organize the next day's floor fight.

"Come back after the dry run," he said brusquely. It was 9:00 P.M. and Kennedy's floor managers and state delegate whips (I was one of them) had gathered in the empty convention hall to test the communications nets that would control Monday's maneuvers.

The rehearsal lasted two hours. Afterward, Wagner still kept putting us off. I decided we would stand outside the trailer until sunrise to make our case.

Finally, at about 1:00 A.M., Wagner led us over to an empty locker room in the Garden. We unfolded metal chairs and sat down in a circle – Rosenfield, Franchot, and I facing Wagner and several of his aides, all of us bone tired.

I explained our case. The Democratic National Committee had turned down our request for speaking time. I only wanted ten minutes of prime time before the delegates to talk about energy and nuclear power. In no way, I emphasized, would it embarrass Kennedy or affect his candidacy. The order is out among Kennedy delegates not to touch the petition. "All we want you to do is tell them they can sign."

Wagner didn't mince his words. "I understand what you are doing," he said quietly. "I sympathize with what you are doing. My problem is, I can't give the senator's approval."

"Carl, no one has supported the senator more than I have," I said. "I'm in a vulnerable position." That was an understatement. I wasn't sure I would escape Madison Square Garden with my scalp. By Sunday night, we already had reached the point of no return. The petitions were all over town waiting to be signed. The press and the networks had been notified we were on our way to Carter with the threat of busting up Thursday night's proceedings. Now we had a potential fiasco on our hands with only one-third of the names we needed on paper.

"Give us six industrial states," I said. "Six states, that's all we need. We'll go to those states, collect our signatures quietly and discreetly."

Wagner thought for a moment.

"I don't really want to do this," he finally said, "But I'll tell you what. I'm meeting with the senator at six o'clock in the morning. I'll recommend to him that he free up some of the large states. If he approves, have your people here at eight o'clock with the names of the states."

The meeting ended, and Franchot hurried over to CSE headquarters to pick the states we wanted freed. Monday morning he handed the list to Wagner, who agreed to allow those delegates to sign. Early Monday afternoon, CSE teams marched out again to the six designated states.

But by late afternoon, calls began pouring into CSE headquarters from frustrated volunteers. No one will sign on, they complained. Whether it was a breakdown in communications or that Wagner was simply too busy to contact the delegations, we never knew. We could not find Wagner, and it was too late to ring up anyone else in the Kennedy trailer to free the delegates, for in less than an hour the open convention debate would begin. Again, the petition drive was dead in the water.

While I raced around the convention floor campaigning for Kennedy, Franchot, Rosenfield, and Phelps sat gloomily in front of a TV set to watch the rules fight and the long, drawn-out roll call vote. The only hope now was that after the open convention vote, perhaps the more antinuclear of Kennedy's delegates would feel free to sign. But, after two days of having doors slammed in their faces, no one was optimistic.

Later that evening, House Speaker O'Neill announced the tally on Kennedy's Rules Minority Report No. 5: 1,936 opposed, 1,390 in favor. The open convention proposal was beaten by a margin almost double that which Carter's men had predicted. Kennedy appeared before the television cameras at the Waldorf-Astoria to tell his supporters what he had already telephoned to Carter at Camp David — he was pulling out of the race.

"Well, that's it," Franchot said, switching off the TV and turning to Rosenfield. The CSE hotel room, for the first time in two days, was quiet.

But not for long.

At about 11:00 P.M., CSE's phones began to ring off their hooks. Soon volunteers rushed in the room with stacks of petitions. Kennedy's delegates were signing on by the droves!

Many of them, angry over losing the rules fight, had stormed out of Madison Square Garden. When CSE teams stopped them, they grabbed the petition sheets and scribbled down their names. The ban was lifted. Kennedy's delegates no longer saw any reason to turn us down. CSE worked almost round the clock wandering down hallways, knocking on doors, grabbing delegates in lobbies.

Yes, there were delegates who saw this as a parting shot at Carter. There were also hundreds of delegates who did not know me from Adam but who were willing to stand up and say, I will sign this fellow's vice presidential papers so he can get up and address the issue of nuclear power at this convention because I think it is that important.

By Tuesday evening we had 645 signatures, almost one-fifth of the convention delegates. As Symons, our other lawyer from Congress Watch, ironed out with the Democratic National Committee the procedural details of filing for vice president, Rosenfield began telephoning Carter headquarters to set up a meeting.

That night, Kennedy gave the best speech of his life, summoning passionately the Democratic Party's New Deal concern for the little guy and attacking lustily the zaniest of Ronald Reagan's campaign statements. "We must not permit the Republicans to seize and run on the slogans of prosperity," the Senator roared to one standing ovation after another. "We heard the orators at their convention all trying to talk like Democrats. They proved that even Republican nominees can quote Franklin Roosevelt to their own purpose."

Afterward, Rick Sterns, Kennedy's chief issues adviser, telephoned to invite me to a late-night supper the senator was having in his hotel suite with about twenty of his inner circle to celebrate his convention speech.

I finally got in touch with White House aide Greg Schneiders, whose brother had served with me in the Massachusetts legislature. Schneiders agreed to meet our negotiating team that night to work out a speaking time.

At 10:30 P.M., while I ate dinner with Kennedy at the Waldorf, Peter Franchot, Harvey Rosenfield, and Doug Phelps crossed the inner perimeter of the Carter command post next to the Garden. Schneiders sat down with Marty Franks from the Carter-Mondale campaign committee. Two hours later, Franchot telephoned me at my room.

"We don't have a time slot," he said nervously.

"What the hell happened!" I shouted.

"Harvey laid out our position," Franchot began. Rosenfield told them that CSE had more than enough signatures to put my name in nomination and that we'd drop our effort of running Ed Markey for vice president in exchange for ten minutes of prime time Wednesday.

Let's get a few things straight from the start, Franks said. Markey is a Kennedy supporter. This is Carter country now. Markey is antinuclear and if anything we're pronuclear. And you want to get up and speak on the night the President is being nominated. If you knew how much you were asking for, how many governors and U.S. senators have asked to speak, and we've turned them down, you'd be embarrassed to ask us. Besides, we don't think Markey will dare to run for vice president. But if you want to let your boss make a fool of himself, go right ahead. He'll be seen as a flake!

Rosenfield, to whom we had delegated total authority in the negotiations, stood firm.

We're going to go forward on this, he said coolly. And if you think we'll bail out, you're making a big mistake.

Schneiders interceded. Now look, we can work something out on this, he said. We'll compromise and give you 10 minutes at 7:15 P.M.

No dice, Rosenfield said. The networks don't turn their cameras on until 7:30; we would not have any coverage at 7:15.

But Campaign for Safe Energy told us they wanted ten minutes of prime time anywhere between 7:00 and 10:00, Schneiders and Franks complained; 7:15 is between those times.

I don't care what CSE told you, Rosenfield said, 7:15 is not prime time.

The five of them spent the next fifteen minutes arguing over the definition of prime time. But Rosenfield would not budge. The meeting broke up about midnight. Schneiders told Rosenfield to come back Wednesday at 8 A.M. and he would give him his final decision.

Franchot, Phelps, and Rosenfield then walked quickly through the almost empty convention hall to an exit. "Okay, let's find Symons and get those signatures submitted right away," Rosenfield said.

"Do you think we should have accepted the 7:15 slot?" Franchot asked.

"Absolutely not!" Rosenfield shot back. "They'll give us what we want. We just have to keep up the pressure."

While Franchot returned to the hotel room to phone me with the news, Rosenfield tracked down Symons, who walked back to the convention secretary's office with the 645 signatures.

As of 12:10 A.M., August 13, 1980, Edward J. Markey from the State of Massachusetts was a candidate for vice president of the United States.

Late the next morning, I was picking at my breakfast in the hotel's coffee shop when I heard my name paged for a phone call.

"Is that you Ed?" Rosenfield asked, out of breath on the other end of the line.

"What's up?"

"You're on at 7:45 tonight!"

"Great! What did they say?"

"I met Franks and had him put it all down in writing. You speak at 7:45 after Governor John Brown of Kentucky and before Max Cleland, the head of the Veterans Administration."

"Fine. Tell Symons to wait until after I've given the speech before he withdraws my nomination."

I rushed back upstairs to tell the rest of my staff we had won. The on-again-off-again speech was on!

Now we had another problem. We had all been so busy finagling time to speak, we had neglected one important item – the speech. I had not even thought about it the past four days.

In eight hours, I would be addressing the largest media fishbowl in the world – 25,000 delegates, alternates, reporters, and government officials, every Democratic congressman, senator, and governor – and I did not have a final draft that CSE liked, the Solar Lobby liked, or I liked.

If we had not been so preoccupied with collecting signatures and negotiating for air time, we would have had the speech completed. We would have spent this time strolling about the convention advertising the speech. We would have called Hal Bruno at ABC and brought him up to date. I would have gotten back to NBC's Chris Wallace and Tom Brokaw, whom I had put on hold when they asked me about my candidacy. Instead, for the next six hours, I was holed up in my hotel room with my staff, CSE, and the Solar Lobby, trying to come up with an acceptable draft.

Different factions pushed different emphases for the ten-minute address. CSE wanted reactors shut down, so it pressed for a strong anti-nuclear statement. The Solar Lobby, not focused on nuclear power, wanted the speech tilted toward solar power.

But I wanted nuclear proliferation in that speech, too. The speech already had what I had said about nuclear power before – that it was not safe, not needed, and not cheap. But for the first time, I wanted my antinuclear speech to say what I now firmly believed: Nuclear reactors are potential nuclear bomb factories and that is the greatest danger nuclear power poses for the world. This is why I support solar power. This is why I want nuclear plants phased out. Because I do not want nuclear war.

Although Tarapur was too specific an incident to include in this type of address, the uranium shipment battle nevertheless helped build the inner momentum to fight our way to the podium. The dangers of nuclear proliferation had to be in the speech, I insisted, and we should not worry about any political backlash from including it.

I had already tested the proliferation argument before a smaller audience in June, when CSE asked me to speak before the Platform Committee in favor of its phaseout plank. I had my standard speech against nuclear power before me, but instead of reading it verbatim, as my staff expected, I boiled it down and, for the last five minutes of my allotted time, took off extemporaneously about how nuclear power leads to nuclear proliferation and nuclear bombs. When I did this, I could feel the mood in the room change. Nuclear bombs struck a chord. The committee members – feminists, Hispanics, blacks, party officials – realized this was an issue they had not begun to consider. As I folded my notes, about ten delegates surrounded me, telling me they agreed with me on the issue. Their response convinced me that the time was ripe for a public dialogue on nuclear proliferation.

For six hours now at the convention, we pored over the draft, haggling over themes, style, metaphors, words. Do we say nuclear power is a "financial turkey?" No, too slangy. "Financial disaster" was penciled in.

Tempers began to flare. Nancy McNary, my press secretary, was pulling her hair out trying to pry a final draft loose from us to circulate among reporters ahead of time.

"Tell Ed Markey to get over here right now!" she finally screamed into a phone from the convention floor at six o'clock. "I've got two Boston TV stations all set up here waiting to interview him!"

The interviews had to be cancelled. David Hoffman, my issues adviser and speechwriter, had just typed the final draft and I had not even read it through once.

At 7:05 P.M., Franchot, Hoffman, and I piled into a cab and sped off to the Garden.

As it turned out, we had plenty of time. The convention was far behind schedule, so I spent an hour and a half in a waiting room with

Franchot, rehearsing my speech and building up my confidence. Even if half of them would not be listening, this was still the largest audience I had ever faced.

Finally, at about 8:45 P.M., I was ushered up to the podium. San Francisco Mayor Dianne Feinstein introduced me. The convention band played *Yankee Doodle Dandy*. About 100 CSE volunteers we had sneaked in whipped out banners and "No Nuke" signs and screamed their heads off for our brief demonstration. And the Massachusetts delegation, seated just in front of the podium, stared up wide eyed.

I shuffled my papers (we did not even have time to put the speech on the teleprompter) and began:

Thank you, Madam Chairman. I am honored to be here tonight to address the Democratic Convention on the issue of nuclear power, the issue of solar power, and a safe, new energy future for America.

The Democratic Platform which we adopted this week now calls for the phaseout of all nuclear power plants in the United States, and a phase-in of a non-nuclear energy future, energy conservation, clean coal, and solar power in all its forms.

As Senator Kennedy declared last night, and I quote, "We can be proud of our Party's stand for investment in safe energy instead of a nuclear future that may threaten the future itself."

I stand here tonight for the tens of millions of Americans who want this energy message to resound across this land. Americans know that a new energy vision will not emerge from the Republican Party. The Republican platform shortchanges solar power and energy conservation. Instead, the Party of Ronald Reagan trumpets the policies of big oil and nuclear companies and mistakes that have been repeated for years. They ignore the promise of a safe energy future. They promote nuclear power as a panacea. They disregard the environment, and they put profit before the public interest.

In November there will be a clear choice between Democrats and Republicans on the issue of a new energy future for America, and Republicans will lose that battle in November because the American people want their future based on solar power, not upon nuclear power.

The American people know, after Three Mile Island, that nuclear power is not failsafe; accidents do happen; and a single accident could kill thousands. The American people know there is no real solution to the problem of radioactive waste, a threat to the health of this and future generations. And as the waste keeps piling up, scientists scratch their heads and wonder what to do.

And nuclear power is not cheap. Even Wall Street knows it is a financial disaster. Reactors that cost $200 million to build only a few years ago now cost well over $1 billion.

Furthermore, nuclear power is not needed. Demand for electricity has dropped sharply. Most of the country has excess capacity, and we are learning that nuclear power does not significantly reduce our dependence upon foreign oil. Only ten percent of our oil is burned to generate electricity.

And perhaps *most alarming of all*, nuclear power guarantees the spread of atomic arms around the world as country after country takes the fuel from their reactors and uses it for weapons. For the same nuclear reactor that boils water to create electricity also creates plutonium, from which the next Ayatollah can roll the dice and hold the entire world hostage.

For all these reasons, millions of Americans will cheer the fact that the Democratic Party has endorsed an orderly phaseout of every nuclear power plant in America, and the fact that the Democratic Party endorses an energy agenda based on conservation and solar power.

In the five years after the 1973 oil embargo, energy conservation and energy efficiency alone delivered two and one-half times the energy of all other energy sources combined, from the Alaskan pipeline, off-shore drilling, nuclear power, all of them. If we saved only 15 percent of our energy today, it would equal all the oil we now import from OPEC. If we launched a crash energy productivity program, we could save millions of barrels of oil every day by 1990, by weatherizing our homes and offices and factories, by tough new appliances and automobile fuel efficiency standards, by industrial innovation and co-generation, not by sacrifice of our living standard, not by a loss of jobs, but simply by investing in the steps already within our reach, to use our energy more wisely.

But saving energy is not enough. We must produce new energy as well. We must accelerate clean coal technology, compatible with environmental quality.

We must drill for new oil and gas. And we must depend upon the sun, for our nation is not running out of energy. Bountiful resources lie all around us, waiting to be tapped—clean, safe, inexhaustible solar energy in all of its forms.

Solar energy is not only the promise of tomorrow, it is here today. Three thousand homes in America now have solar equipment on their roofs. Thousands have woodburning stoves in their dens and living rooms. Thousands of farms are turning crops into gasohol. Dozens of cities are burning their trash to produce electric power. Hundreds of streams and rivers have been harnessed to produce electricity, and thousands of businesses produce wind machines and solar collectors to draw power from the sun—power from the sun that is immune to boycotts and embargoes, power from the sun that will leave our earth unravaged.

Within 20 years, renewable resources could deliver more than one-quarter of our nation's energy, and within 50 years we could be a truly solar society.

Americans will pitch in. They will roll up their sleeves, like the people of Davis, California; like the people of Fitchburg in my own State of Massachusetts, where everyone last year, from senior citizens to school children, launched a campaign to weatherize every one of Fitchburg's 14,000 homes; like the delegates who came here to this convention, working with the Campaign for Safe Energy and the Solar Lobby, to demand that the Democratic Party take an important first step toward the charting of this new energy vision for America.

In our Democratic Platform, we have promised to phase out, as alternatives are ready, all nuclear plants in this nation. We have promised to fight for more dollars to speed the arrival of a solar tomorrow, to bring it within the reach of every American.

But we need more than just words in our platform. Words can just be a sop to the discontented. We must leave this convention determined to go the full distance, to ensure that these pledges are fulfilled because history will record that the challenge of shaping a new and a safe and a more secure energy future was the great challenge of the 1980s. The Republican Party platform points in one direction, but it is a discredited direction, a direction of the past, for they are the party of nostalgia. But for the people of this country, the past is just a memory, and the future is their hard reality.

The decisions before us are as urgent as any that have faced us in our 200-year history. The United States can no longer tolerate to have the course of its energy destiny being set by the oil tankers of OPEC. Our nation's survival hangs in the balance.

But we can meet this challenge. Let us join together, let us shape together a new energy destiny for this country, breaking our addiction on imported oil, phasing out of nuclear power, and committed to leading America and the world into the solar age.

Thank you very much.[4]

All things considered, it was not a bad speech. But there was another problem.

Under the new convention rules, a presidential candidate was required to pledge in writing that he would support the party platform and list any objections he had. This statement had to be in the delegates' hands before the nomination vote. Carter, for example, was not enthusiastic about a $12 billion jobs program plank Kennedy had pushed through, nor a feminist plank that cut off party money to Democratic candidates who did not support the Equal Rights Amendment. These or any other reservations had to be on paper and before the delegates so the President could be nominated.

Coincidentally, just as I began my speech, Stuart Eizenstat released Carter's platform statement.

CBS, NBC, and ABC quickly turned their cameras away from the podium to their correspondents on the convention floor, who were grabbing union chiefs and NOW leaders, shoving microphones into their faces for comments on the Carter statement. If you strained, you could hear my voice in the background as Gloria Steinem chewed out the President for waffling on the ERA plank. But that was it. None of the three networks carried the speech. The issue of nuclear power and nuclear proliferation never reached past the walls of the convention hall to the American public.

"The will is infinite," wrote William Shakespeare, "and the execution confined."

7

The Just Barely Nuclear Congress

The Committee Votes

The House Foreign Affairs Committee and the Senate Foreign Relations Committee met on September 10 to decide their recommendations for the two Tarapur export licenses. They were votes no one except us particularly wanted – especially not the congressional leadership, which was unenthusiastic about having two export licenses to Tarapur become the watershed of nonproliferation policy. Compromise, compromise. There must be a way to compromise so the Nonproliferation Act would not be put on the chopping block.

A variety of compromises were kicked around. Congressman Bingham, for example, proposed that the first shipment, the one applied for earlier, be sent; Congress would disapprove the second one "at this time, but without prejudice to its resubmission by the Administration."[1] The first shipment's nineteen tons of uranium would be enough to keep Tarapur operating into the mid-1980s. The Administration thus would have time to negotiate with India to adopt full-scope safeguards before she needed the other nineteen tons. If India proved willing, the other export license could be resubmitted to the Hill for approval.

The White House also cooked up a compromise, if you could call it that. Congress would approve *both* shipments; but the Administration would hold the second shipment until Tarapur needed it. Before the second shipment left, the Administration would *consult* Congress on the progress made in persuading India to agree to the Nonproliferation Act's provisions. The second nineteen tons would not be shipped if India exploded a bomb or was preparing to do so. This, in effect, was no compromise at all, Bingham complained, since Congress would retain no power to review and pass on the later shipment.

As far as we were concerned, all compromise proposals dealt a body blow to nonproliferation because they carved out an exception for one of the worst offenders. Granted, the legislative process hinges on compromises of details and subtle changes in wording, but by even suggesting a compromise, the powerbrokers on Capitol Hill allowed themselves to be trapped in the State Department legal minutiae, which only weakened opposition to Tarapur. Why compromise on the House side, we further argued, when everyone's tally showed that chamber overwhelmingly opposed to shipping any of the uranium? Glenn, to his credit, also took the hard line in the Senate.

Besides, all this talk of compromise was one-sided; there was not a scintilla of evidence that India's intransigence over the Nonproliferation Act had softened. If anything, she rattled her saber during the Tarapur debate. A spokesman for India's External Affairs Ministry told the Associated Press on June 21 that India still reserved the right to conduct nuclear explosions. About a month later, Indira Gandhi proudly announced that India had orbited a 77-pound satellite with a rocket that eventually could be developed into an intercontinental ballistic missile.

So by September 10, the lines were drawn. Carter demanded an all-or-nothing passage; Glenn stood fast with his resolution of disapproval, as did Bingham, who had become peeved by White House stubbornness on Tarapur; we had been itching for a fight from the beginning; and the press was clamoring for a resolution of disapproval.

"To sell uranium now to defiant India would risk the collapse of practical efforts to limit nuclear weapons, there and elsewhere," *The New York Times* editorialized the day before the committee votes. "President Carter seems ready to take that risk. We hope Congress is not."[2]

The House Foreign Affairs Committee

The House Foreign Affairs Committee met at 9:30 A.M. and, to no one's surprise, voted in favor of Bingham's resolution to disapprove the uranium shipments. Yet, even though we had won in the House committee, the vote was disappointing because it was a voice vote.

The voice vote, we learned later, was a compromise the Foreign Affairs Committee leadership had agreed to at the White House's urging. Everyone knew Foreign Affairs would come down against the President by a wide margin. That margin, we felt, would provide crucial momentum to bolster the weaker opposition on the Senate Foreign Relations Committee. With only a voice vote, all Senate Foreign Relations knew was that House Foreign Affairs opposed the shipment; it did not have a roll call vote to indicate how solidly opposed Foreign Affairs was. To diffuse the momentum, the White House lobbied for a voice vote, so its defeat before Foreign Affairs could thus be interpreted as anywhere from overwhelming to slim. Assuming that Glenn's disapproval resolution had no chance in the Senate Foreign Relations Committee, where the State Department's headcount had nine of the committee's fifteen senators voting with the Administration, the House Foreign Affairs leadership decided not to bruise an incumbent president further with a roll call vote. But Foreign Affairs may have been premature in writing the Glenn resolution's obituary.

The Senate Foreign Relations Committee

About a half-hour after the House committee vote, Secretary of State Edmund S. Muskie was closeted in executive session with his former colleagues on the Senate Foreign Relations Committee to discuss what Church claimed were "confidential aspects of the Tarapur issue." Actually, the closed-door meeting was nothing more than an old fashioned arm-twisting session, and an extraordinary one at that.

Realizing that the Senate offered the best chance for victory, the State Department, White House, and Church had been intensively lobbying the fifteen members of Foreign Relations. And Muskie became the most enthusiastic latecomer to the Administration assault team.

The new secretary publicly admitted that initially he had misgivings about the Administration's position on Tarapur. Muskie had long been a nonproliferation advocate in the Senate and many of the staffers he took from the Hill to State reportedly opposed having their boss buckle to the Administration's position.

But when Muskie climbed on board, he did so with pressure tactics that would make a Texas oil lobbyist blush. To have the Secretary of State up on the Hill—one hour before a Foreign Relations Committee vote—cajoling and pleading with Senators in a back room to support the White House on Tarapur was unprecedented.

Shortly after 11 A.M., ten members of Foreign Relations—Democrats Church, Glenn, Claiborne Pell of Rhode Island, Joseph Biden of Delaware, and Paul Sarbanes of Maryland; Republicans Percy, Jacob Javits of New York, Jesse Helms of North Carolina, S. I. Hayakawa of California, and Richard Lugar of Indiana – filed into the committee's main hearing room, which was packed with spectators and press. I had sent Franchot over to monitor the proceedings and report back to me.

Church opened the hearing with an exchange of letters between him and Muskie, which purported to demonstrate to the opposition that Carter was willing to bend on Tarapur.

Church produced a letter he had given Muskie asking that the Administration agree to a compromise. But Church's compromise turned out to be nothing more than the Administration's compromise – that is, Congress would approve both shipments, but the White House would delay delivering the second shipment until Tarapur needed it, and would merely consult Congress before the second nineteen tons were sent.[3]

Church next read Muskie's response in a letter the secretary had hand delivered that morning. Muskie, of course, found Church's compromise "acceptable."[4]

"The Tarapur issue has been very troubling to me," Church continued. "It is classically a question of which there are powerful arguments on both sides. The Administration has given us strong foreign policy, security and nonproliferation reasons why the exports should be approved. Senator Glenn and others have described forcefully why, in their judgment, approval would damage the credibility of U.S. non-proliferation policy. I would say whichever way one comes out, the decision has to be a close one.

"In coming to my own position on Tarapur, I have tried to step back from the myriad of technical ánd legal details and to weigh the broad policy questions. I would like to review briefly why, after considering these policy questions, and with this exchange of letters, I believe that overall U.S. interests are best served by approving the licenses." Church then repeated the State Department debating points.

"Therefore, I am willing to give the Administration another opportunity to see whether India is willing to strengthen its nonproliferation policies and commitments," he said. "I came to this conclusion because I believe the Nonproliferation Act and the full-scope safeguards requirement remain credible and on that basis I am prepared to support the President's position.

"I know there are other points of view to be expressed this morning. First of all I would like, Senator Javits, to ask if you would like to speak on the subject."

"Mr. Chairman, we are on a vote," Glenn interrupted. "I wonder what is the intent of the chairman? I have a lot of material here I wanted to present to the committee before we have a vote. I know you had expressed yourself previously as hoping to have a vote by twelve o'clock. That is going to give me all of about three minutes to put in an awful lot of material."

"We will give you reasonable time," Church assured Glenn. "I would hope that after the discussion by the committee we could come to a vote whenever that is."

"You do plan to vote today?" Glenn asked, politely, but firmly.

"I think members have been put on notice that we will vote," Church answered.

"What is the cutoff date?" Glenn persisted.

"I will assure the senator that he will have adequate time to present his case," Church said. "Senator Javits, do you have a statement?"

Javits announced he would back the Administration and vote against Glenn's disapproval resolution; however, he cautioned that he reserved the right to change his mind when the full Senate voted.

"At a time when so many of our alliances are in disarray – even in our NATO alliance – it seems to me unwise to jeopardize yet another with the second most populous nation in the world," Javits said. "It is an important interest of ours" to maintain close ties with the free world "and this looks to me like a litmus paper test for India with us. We are not free from other controversies, no major power would be, but I believe this one should not be faced at this time."

The committee recessed briefly for an unrelated floor vote. When it reassembled, Glenn presented the opposition's side by first throwing cold water on the Church-Muskie letter exchange.

All the Administration agreed to in its compromise proposal is "that there would be no export of the fuel before it is needed on the second shipment; but there is no question at all as to whether [the Administration] would actually go ahead with it, whether it would be right or not," he said. "So I don't really see that as being any big step forward. . . . We are also putting on the caveat that there may be no nuclear device planned, or that we know of. I would submit that that is a very thin reed to try to hang on." The United States was caught off guard when India exploded its first bomb, he pointed out. Now under the Administration's compromise, the United States would rely again on the same intelligence-gathering apparatus that apparently was inadequate in 1974.

Realizing that with the committee's ranking members supporting Carter the odds were stacked against him, Glenn spent the next fifteen minutes going through all the reasons he could think of why India should not receive the uranium."We will have undermined the policy and removed the standard that we worked so hard to establish two years ago if this committee and the Congress allows this to happen," he concluded. "We send a signal to everyone that it is business as usual again, that nuclear trade in the absence of safeguards is once again the norm for the world and is now considered the respectable way to do business by the United States.

"It seems to me that future generations will look back at this time period and we may have a lot to answer for."

Percy spoke next. Reminding Glenn that he, too, helped draft the 1978 Nonproliferation Act, Percy insisted they have the same goal. "I just respectfully disagree with the way we should carry out these goals," he said. "I think this action by us under these circumstances, the very clouded circumstances that we face and the gray areas of this agreement, would label us as an unreliable supplier. I think it would set back enormously the cause of nonproliferation. The best argument that Senator Glenn has used is that there would be worldwide concern about the United States if we didn't implement our own act.

"I spent one week in Geneva. Forty nations met privately . . . and discussed this particular issue. I found not a single nation, including the major countries, that took the position that in this case, under these circumstances, we should forego this shipment or deny these applications that have been made.

"I therefore intend to vote against the resolution of disapproval on the sale of nuclear fuel for India, not only on this committee but also on the floor of the Senate."

Hayakawa then dropped a bombshell.

Back in May, the State Department, working through the Foreign Relations Committee staff, had touched bases with one of Hayakawa's staff members on how the California senator would vote. Hayakawa was with the Administration on this one, the staffer reported. That person, however, later moved on and his replacement, who held different views about Tarapur, convinced Hayakawa that the White House should be opposed. State never checked back with the senator to make sure his vote was still firm.

"I . . . intend to support Senator Glenn without making commitment as to my ultimate vote on the floor," he told his fellow committee members. "I am most concerned about the fact that we are overruling the decision of the Nuclear Regulatory Commission."

The 9 to 6 vote the Administration forecast was whittled down to 8 to 7; still a majority for the White House, but now a slim one that set State's officials in the audience nervously whispering to one another.

"No further debate being called for, the clerk will call the roll," Church instructed.

Pell's was the first name read, and he dropped the second bombshell. Although he was considered a close call, the White House thought that the Rhode Island senator would be with it on this one. But when the clerk asked for his vote on Glenn's disapproval resolution, Pell in a clear voice said, "Aye."

Pell had changed his mind. He was backing Glenn!

The clerk proceeded.

George McGovern of South Dakota – aye, announced Glenn, who had his proxy.

Biden – no.

Glenn – aye.

Richard Stone of Florida – aye by proxy, Glenn said.

Sarbanes – no.

Edward Zorinsky of Nebraska – no by proxy, Church announced.

Paul Tsongas of Massachusetts – absent, and no one had his proxy.

Javits – no.

Percy – no.

Howard Baker, then the Senate Minority Leader – no by proxy, said Church.

Helms – aye.

Hayakawa – aye.

Lugar – aye.

Church – no.

With the gallery buzzing, the committee staff quickly totaled the votes.

A 7 to 7 tie!

Paul Tsongas had not yet voted. He was busy chairing a subcommittee hearing in another part of the Dirksen Senate Office Building.

A Glenn staff man bolted out the back door.

Both Church and Glenn had lobbied Tsongas heavily and Glenn's staff believed the Massachusetts senator leaned toward opposing the Tarapur shipment.

Smelling victory, Glenn grabbed the microphone.

"Can we have unanimous consent that the vote be kept open until we poll the members?" he asked Church hoping to stall for time while his staff hunted down Tsongas.

But Church also had a victory in his grasp if he could close the vote before Tsongas arrived. A tie vote would mean the disapproval resolution was defeated.

"That would change the rule of the committee," he told Glenn. "If I understand it, that is a practice in the case where it will not change the result of the vote. The vote is 7 to 7."

"Mr. Chairman, what is our time limit on taking this vote?" Glenn asked, the tension building in the committee room.

"The vote has been taken and it is 7 to 7," Church said.

"Mr. Chairman, I would submit that we have another member and we can certainly give him a couple of minutes to get here," Glenn said, leaning forward and glaring at Church.

Javits tried to run interference for Church, shifting the committee's attention to an anti-tariff waiver he had on the calendar.

"Is there objection to the motion of Senator Javits? Without objection, the waiver will be approved," Church said quickly, ignoring Glenn, who appeared ready to leap out of his chair and throw it across the room.

"Mr. Chairman," he said, his face getting redder by the minute. "I would move the adoption of the . . ."

"Let's proceed in regular fashion on this," Church interrupted testily, "and then you can move to reconsider and that would give some opportunity. I think that the regular order in the rules of the committee should be upheld."

"Mr. Chairman, I would object!"

By Foreign Relations' genteel standards, this squabble was beginning to turn into a barroom brawl.

"I would object very strongly!" Glenn continued, becoming angrier and angrier. "I have been in many committee meetings where we have bent over backwards to let the committee members get to the room and vote!"

"Senator Glenn, there is no effort on my part to prevent members from getting here," Church snapped. "I say the vote has been taken. The vote is 7 to 7, and the chair announces a tie vote!"

"I object!"

Biden, who had sided with Church, finally stepped in to cool tempers and asked that the vote remain open since Tsongas reportedly was on his way up the stairs.

Franchot, who had slipped out of the committee room, was pacing back and forth when Tsongas came racing down the hallway. Out of breath, the Massachusetts senator entered through the rear door of the committee room. He scanned the crowd, then walked to his seat.

Church turned to his left.

"Do you wish to vote at this time?" he asked.

"Yes, Aye," Tsongas replied.

"You do," Church said, and just to make sure, he added, "You wish to vote, and your vote is aye."

"Yes."

Reporters streamed out of the committee room.

Church slumped back in his chair.

"That makes the total 8 ayes and 7 nays and the resolution of disapproval is recommended by the committee to the Senate," he sighed.[5]

The Floor Votes

The upset left everyone dazed. The White House had confidently calculated that a Foreign Relations Committee win would be enough to kill Glenn's disapproval resolution on the floor, while the most we had ever hoped for was that damage from Foreign Relations might be contained when the full Senate voted. Now the White House was on the defensive. Glenn had punctured enemy lines. We now had to regroup quickly for the offensive.

Some reconnoitering that afternoon revealed that the House Foreign Affairs Committee was not pressing for a quick House vote. Perhaps because it assumed that Glenn's resolution had no chance in the Senate and that any House action would eventually become moot, House Foreign Affairs never fought Tarapur as aggressively as we would have liked. Now we had a horse race to produce a House vote and victory first, thus creating some momentum for the Senate vote, whose outcome, everyone realized, was much less predictable.

The White House, it turns out, had a similar strategy in place for the Senate. Convinced that Glenn's disapproval resolution would never make it past Foreign Relations, the Administration had arranged for a Senate vote almost immediately after the hearing. Glenn's forces would be in disarray after a committee defeat; therefore, Carter wanted a Senate vote before Tarapur's opposition had time to reassemble. Also, the President only needed one chamber to approve the shipment. If the Senate voted first, and upheld his decision, Carter would have let the air out of a House decision.

But with Foreign Relations now voting the other way, handing Glenn the momentum, the President had to backtrack. His men scrambled up to the Hill to plead with the Senate leadership for a delay. The leadership allowed the Administration a two-week postponement of the vote. The concession proved crucial, for it permitted the White House and State Department more time to lobby.

The Tarapur Lobbies

Lobbying has been a cozy part of lawmaking ever since seventeenth century supplicants cornered British legislators in lobbies of Parliament (from which the term is derived). And, as with other controversies, Tarapur produced its special brand of lobbying. Tarapur was notable by the fact that the two major groups normally out in full force on other nuclear issues, the antinuclear lobbies and the pronuclear industry lobbies, remained largely silent.

Part of the inactivity can be attributed to the issue. Tarapur was an upper-echelon, foreign policy debate that never stretched beyond the State Department, the Hill, or the editorial boards to the grass roots. Another factor was the nature of the lobbies.

ANTINUCLEAR LOBBY

In the case of antinuclear lobbies, resources and priorities limited their involvement. Public interest and environmental groups in Washington are chronically unprosperous, understaffed, and uncoordinated. Consequently, they set priorities, target issues for lobbying, and unfortunately often work at cross-purposes. With not enough manpower to visit each office personally, they resort to mass mailings or to lobbying a few opinion makers. The goal of the pinpoint lobbying is favorable editorials by major newspapers. But on Tarapur, three important publications, *The New York Times, The Washington Post,* and *The Wall Street Journal,* had joined the fray long ago, as had almost one hundred other papers across the country. And, save for a few that circulated letters, public interest groups, by and large, never stuffed the mailboxes opposing Tarapur—for philosophical and political reasons.

If a nuclear waste disposal bill came up for a vote or Metropolitan Edison tried to crank up Three Mile Island's Unit-2 or the American Nuclear Energy Council wanted more Department of Energy subsidies for reactor manufacturers, groups like the Sierra Club and Congress Watch would be swarming all over the Hill. Nuclear proliferation, however, does not stir many coals.

The issue of nuclear proliferation, by the time of the Tarapur vote, was still relegated to the important-but-not-now status. I do not mean this to be an indictment of the lobby. Public interest and environmental groups are creatures of the concerned citizens who pay their dues. The movement follows the public, which, up to this point, worried about plant safety issues raised by Three Mile Island.

The 75,000 who gathered on the Mall in Washington a year before waved their "No Nuke" signs because they were afraid of reactor core meltdowns and radiation discharges, not because they were afraid of the bomb. They may have favored nuclear disarmament, but I could probably count on my hands the ban-the-bomb advocates among them who, like the children of the 1950s, protested atomic power's link with atomic weapons.

Their numbers were few partly out of design. A sharp split existed in the antinuclear movement between people who were concerned about nuclear power and peace groups opposed to nuclear bombs. The people concerned about nuclear power – the traditional antinukers who make up most of the movement – have resisted admitting peace groups to their coalition. The reason is political. The antinuclear movement in 1980 had more than 60 percent public support – both liberal and conservative – when it focused its rhetoric on safety-related issues such as Three Mile Island. The minute the ban-the-bomb and peace people stepped in, conservatives drifted away and approval ratings dipped.

Unfortunately, the same animosity is found among the arms control and disarmament groups, whose ranks have swelled in the past year as more people have become concerned about Ronald Reagan's nuclear war fighting rhetoric. The ban-the-bomb groups, which are attracting more members from the business and professional communities, have been cool to the idea of admitting the antinukers. A sizable portion of the disarmament groups' memberships are against nuclear weapons but not against nuclear power.

PRONUCLEAR LOBBY.

The nuclear industry also remained in the background on Tarapur for many of the same reasons. On a domestic nuclear question, the pronuke lobby will arrange for utility company officials in a congressman's home district to telephone him and push the industry's case. One phone call from a power company executive is worth twenty constituents writing letters. It is very effective.

The nuclear lobby, however, prefers to avoid international proliferation issues and the mushroom cloud images they evoke. Its cardinal rule: Always distinguish between the peaceful atom and the military one.

Industry intrusion in Tarapur also might have been perceived as an attempt to advance corporate goals at the expense of foreign policy interests. Far better to have the State Department and White House carry industry's water, which both were enthusiastically doing.[a]

The industry did have the services of its two most vociferous pro-

[a]The Indian lobby also did not have to be particularly vigorous because of State Department boosterism. The Indians, for their part, kept pointing to the 1963 agreement and threatening to reprocess Tarapur's spent fuel. India, however, reacted calmly to the committee votes. "These are domestic processes of decision-making within the United States," a spokesman for her Ministry of External Affairs told *The New York Times*.[6] New Delhi's reponse, however, may have worked to the disadvantage of the White House, which had been spreading the word that the Indians would hit the roof if the congressional committees turned them down.

ponents in the House—Congressmen John Wydler of New York and Mike McCormack of Washington.[b] The "nuke twins," as Wydler once called the duo, made a last-minute blitz of Dear Colleagues to stave off defeat in the House.[7] "The NRC's failure to approve the shipment is being used by some anti-nuclear activists (from within the Congress and from outside) as an argument that the Congress should overturn the President's order and prohibit the shipment," McCormack griped in one of his early letters. "Such an impetuous and unthinking act by Congress would serve no constructive purpose, and would be disastrously self-defeating."[8]

But, by and large, the insiders—the major newspapers, the Tarapur opponents on the Hill, and the proponents in the Executive Branch—eclipsed the nuclear industry and antinuclear lobbies.

THE MEDIA LOBBY

How many votes it swayed, nobody knows, but the influence of the media lobby was considerable, particularly among congressional staffs. Leading the editorial effort was *The Washington Post,* which almost monthly strafed the White House with an anti-Tarapur editorial.

"Nuclear cooperation is a two-way street," *The Post* editorialized after the committee votes. While the shipment's backers have been harping on the fact that the United States must remain a reliable nuclear supplier, they have ignored the fact that India has not been a particularly reliable customer.[9]

On September 22, the day before the full Senate began debate on Tarapur, *The Post* drove home the point again with two articles opposing Jimmy Carter. Glenn had a lengthy column on the op ed page, imploring his colleagues to vote against the shipment.

"In 1974, using American-supplied heavy water and a Canadian reactor, India detonated an atomic explosion and thus became the first nation to divert civilian nuclear materials to potential weapon use," Glenn wrote, revealing that "though the State Department now claims the 1974 test violated no commitments, a diplomatic note, recently declassified at my request and delivered to India four years *before* the atomic test, unequivocally declares that the use of U.S. heavy water for nuclear explosions would be a contravention of the terms under which the American materials were made available.'"[10]

"So much for the leverage bought by continuing nuclear supply," *The Post* continued in an editorial on the preceding page. "The Administration is arguing that since India didn't accept the U.S. position stated

[b] McCormack was defeated for reelection in November 1980.

in that document, it never violated an agreement. This is pure Alice in Wonderland: to defend its position now, the U.S. government accepts India's rejection of its earlier position. So much for consistency and firmness of purpose."[11]

Perhaps the most scathing of editorials came from *The Wall Street Journal*, whose opinion carried great weight with Republicans and conservatives on Capitol Hill. "We are now asked to decide whether to give more nuclear materials to the people who used the first ones in ways we prohibited," *The Journal* wrote the day of the Senate vote. "Any President or Senator who has the gall to approve this sale and still say he is opposed to nuclear proliferation should be called to account by the voters in the next election for fecklessness, but even more for hypocrisy."[12]

The media lobbying also came indirectly from the news pages and airwaves. Just before the Senate vote, *The Post* ran a front-page story that said "despite repeated U.S. protests, Switzerland has been knowingly exporting to Pakistan sophisticated nuclear technology that Pakistan is believed to be using to develop an atomic bomb." The Swiss government, *The Post* reported, has allowed several Swiss firms to sell "vital components" to enrich uranium to bomb-usable standards. Fearing a nuclear arms race between India and Pakistan might result in nuclear war between the two countries, the Administration warned the Swiss that their exports undermined efforts to keep atomic weapons out of Pakistani hands. The Swiss responded that the exports, which can be used "for a variety of purposes other than nuclear technology," did not violate any international agreements. "At the same time," *The Post* noted, in a jab at Carter's Tarapur decision, "the United States, among other countries, has shown itself willing to depart from antiproliferation guidelines when it considers this politically useful."[c, 13]

Just before the House vote, Bingham and McCormack appeared in *U.S. News & World Report* in a point-counterpoint:

> **Question:** India has said that if the sale does not go through, it would feel free to use previously supplied uranium for any purpose, including nuclear arms. Wouldn't that be a blow to nonproliferation efforts?
>
> **Bingham:** I think that's a kind of blackmail. The fact is that the [1963] agreement to supply the uranium includes a provision that India will comply with all applicable laws of the United States. Now that means that India is obligated to comply with the Nuclear Nonproliferation Act of 1978, which means allowing inspection of all its nuclear facilities . . .

cThree months later, the Swiss agreed to screen more closely, and possibly ban, the technology exports if the United States would resume its nuclear agreements with Switzerland.

Question: . . . Why are so many members of the Congress prepared to block the fuel sale?

McCormack: I don't think they are. You have no such information. Where there is confusion, it is because the media have not done their job of presenting the facts about nuclear fuels and nuclear energy.

Also, there is a tendency among some not to like the Indians because the Indians have cooperated to some extent with the Russians. And there is some antagonism between India and the United States because too many U.S. public officials assume that we have a right to tell the Indians what to do. They are just as sophisticated and just as independent as we are.[14]

I appeared on public television's "NacNeil/Lehrer Report" for a half-hour debate on Tarapur with NRC Commissioner Victor Gilinsky, Percy, and Charles Van Doren of the U.S. Arms Control and Disarmament Agency.

Robert MacNeil: How do you define the blackmail that you say the Indian government is trying to exercise on us?

Markey: They are saying that we will lose their friendship, that because we are not going to be a reliable supplier . . . we will in some way be jeopardizing our diplomatic relations with them. . . . I think it's incumbent upon us to understand that the Gandhi government— which has engaged in a $1.6 billion arms pact with the Soviets recently, has endorsed the regime in Kampuchea, has begun the negotiations, trade and otherwise with the Iranians in the aftermath of the taking of our hostages—really can't be looked at as someone that has had the long-term best interests of the Americans in their public policy consideration. . . .

Jim Lehrer to Percy: You see it, then, as a breach of contract with India if we do not go ahead (with the shipment).

Percy: Absolutely. I agree with Secretary Muskie, who feels very strongly that we would be in violation of our own contract. . . . I think that every nuclear supplier around the world would want to see us fill this contract and then draw the line. But don't draw the line on a gray area. . . .

MacNeil to Gilinsky: What do you say to Senator Percy's point that (the Indians) applied for this fuel shipment well within the grace period and it was American delay which caused them not to get it?

Gilinsky: The legislative history of the act, it seems to me, makes clear that there was to be a sharp cutoff at the two-year point after the date the act went into effect. There was a delay. I think the reason for the delay on the American side in submitting that application to our commission stemmed from the fact that there was hope that the Indians would be forthcoming and would come to some agreement or make some statement that would limit future development on nuclear explosives. . . .

Lehrer: Along with the State Department, the U.S. Arms Control and Disarmament Agency came down the other way. They recommended and still support sale of the fuel to India. Charles Van Doren is assistant director of the agency for nonproliferation. First, Mr. Van Doren, some find it strange that an agency dedicated to nonproliferation would support the sale of this fuel to a nation that has thumbed its nose at nonproliferation. Why have you taken this position?

Charles Van Doren: Well, first, because we share the view expressed by Senator Percy that the United States should keep its contracts, keep its agreements, and we do not consider that the Nonproliferation Act requires us to do otherwise in this case on these two shipments. And second, we think that there would be a net nonproliferation loss if we refused these shipments.[15]

THE MARKEY LOBBY

In addition to the media campaign, we began churning out Dear Colleagues and Congressional Record inserts the week before the House vote. And, as the day of decision drew near, we introduced the "ayatollah factor."

During the November 1979 debate over my nuclear power plant moratorium amendment, Wydler had a cute ploy to derail our support. The amendment vote occurred about three weeks after Iranian students seized the U.S. Embassy in Tehran. On November 14, Wydler distributed a Dear Colleague that said "the Ayatollah Khomeini will certainly be delighted" if congressmen support the Markey Amendment. A yes vote, Wydler claimed, would "send a clear signal to the terrorists in Iran and to the other Arab OPEC nations that our country lacks the resolve to utilize an available energy resource and is willing to make itself more dependent than ever on Arab oil."[16]

That was enough to scare off some congressmen. The Wydler letter cannot be credited with killing the Moratorium Amendment. The measure still would have failed had there been no Iranian crisis and no letter. The hostage crisis, however, did sap some support for the amendment — much in the same way the crisis became a liability for Senator Kennedy when, one month after the embassy takeover, he was raked over the political coals during his presidential bid for criticizing U.S. support for the Shah of Iran.

The morning of the House vote on Tarapur, we decided to give Wydler a dose of his own medicine. The 435 representatives received from the Markey office a Dear Colleague entitled, "India Aids Iran and Does Not Deserve American Nuclear Fuel."

On the back of the letter we reprinted a June 14 news report out of
New Delhi that India planned to export grain and industrial products to
Iran to help beat U.S. sanctions imposed after the embassy takeover. "I
wonder if our hostages can figure out what broad foreign policy objectives are being met through the sale of uranium to India, a country that
not only refuses to accept full-scope safeguards, but explicitly tries to
undermine our attempt to put pressure on a country such as Iran,
which is actively doing us harm?" I queried.[17] The letter probably did
not have a substantial effect on the outcome of the House vote; but if
Khomeini could frighten some off the Moratorium Amendment he
could do the same with Tarapur.

The Lobby of the House Vote

The House began its debate the morning of September 18. It was an
enjoyable debate, as far as I was concerned. Bingham floor-managed
the resolution, with Zablocki and Broomfield, the top Democrat and
Republican on the Foreign Affairs Committee, behind him. The coalition of House Foreign Affairs Committee leaders, liberal Democrats,
and the Republican right wing formed an unbeatable team.

McCormack and Wydler, accustomed to leading stampedes against
the antinuclear movement, now struggled to hold back the flood of
opposition to Tarapur. And, other than Indiana Congressman Lee
Hamilton, a ranking Democrat on Foreign Affairs who presented State's
arguments, and California Congressman Paul McCloskey, a prominent
House Republican who felt Congress should defer to the President "in
close questions of foreign policy," the pro-Tarapur coalition was notice-
ably short of barons.

The debate was perhaps somewhat useful, but not terribly enlight-
ening; we had been over the arguments pro and con many times before.
No head counts were needed. The Administration had already given up
on the House. The only objective now was to run up the score to
impress the Senate. We also wanted to gain the support of congressmen
from as many states as possible. Senators who came from those states
might look at their congressional delegations to determine if their
positions were compatible.

I leaned back in my seat, watching and waiting for my turn to speak
in a play that had been scripted long before. This was a mop-up
operation.

That afternoon, the House of Representatives voted. Bingham's resolution, disapproving the export of thirty-eight tons of low-enriched
uranium to India, was approved 298 to 98.

For the pronuclear lobby not to win at least 100 votes in a legislative body that had been so generous to it in the past was a sobering experience. A 3-to-1 loss in the House also delivered to Jimmy Carter a stinging defeat whose shockwaves, we hoped, would be felt at the other end of the Capitol. For, in the final analysis, all our work, from the first letter to Carter to the House vote three months later, ended up as one big lobbying effort to sustain the insurrection John Glenn had fomented in the Senate.

During the final days before that chamber's vote, Glenn and his aides dialed office after office to influence resolution opponents and uncommitteds. His lobby and ours, however, paled in comparison to what the Administration launched.

The White House Lobby

Not since Panama Canal had the White House marshaled such a massive effort to shove through a foreign policy measure. Gerard Smith, the State Department's nonproliferation ambassador, and Ralph Earle, director of the Arms Control and Disarmament Agency, practically camped out on the Hill.

"My job is to try to contain the cancerous spread of nuclear weapons around the world," Smith wrote in a letter distributed to every senator a week before the vote. "I have been trying to do this for the last 30 years. If our country terminates its uranium supply to India under an agreement that the Congress reviewed 17 years ago, I think our nonproliferation program will receive a sharp setback."

Muskie also roamed the corridors briefing and breakfasting with old friends and wavering senators on both sides of the aisle. The Maine Democrat even dropped in on the Republican Policy Committee for a bit of bipartisan persuasion.

"The Administration is staging a full-court press," Senator Tsongas marveled in an interview with *The New York Times*.[18] The *Times* also reported that the President lobbied New Jersey Senator Bill Bradley, who remained silent on his position, practically up to the minute he voted. Fellow New Jersey Senator Harrison Williams reportedly was in the middle of a House-Senate conference meeting when the White House patched through a call from Carter. (Bradley voted with the Administration; Williams did not.)[19] Even Secretary of Defense Harold Brown took up phone duty, pleading with old friends on the Hill not to rebuke the President on Tarapur.

But perhaps the best lobbyist in the Administration's stable was a Boeing 707 named "Air Force One." Busy on the campaign trail, Carter telephoned about ten undecided senators from the presidential jet. As Glenn conceded during the Senate Tarapur debate, "It is very impressive to receive a call from Air Force One."[20] And very effective.

The Senate Vote

By the time the Senate got around to debating Tarapur on September 23 and voting on it the morning of September 24, Glenn was lopsidedly outgunned. Senate Majority Leader Robert Byrd and Minority Leader Howard Baker lined up support for the Administration. Percy and Church hammered away at the foreign policy repercussions if the United States turned down India. Javits, Sarbanes, and Henry M. "Scoop" Jackson of Washington recited in eye-watering detail the contractual obligations under the 1963 agreement and the State Department's convoluted interpretation of the 1978 Nonproliferation Act's grace-period provision. Other senators who spoke in support of the Administration included James McClure of Idaho, a ranking Republican on the Energy and Natural Resources Committee and energetic nuclear proponent; Daniel Patrick Moynihan, a New York Democrat and a former ambassador to India; and John Stennis, a Mississippi Democrat and chairman of the Armed Services Committee.

Glenn's bullpen of heavyweights was thin. Senate Majority Whip Alan Cranston spoke out against shipping the uranium, as did Governmental Affairs Committee Chairman Abraham Ribicoff of Connecticut and Republican Robert Dole of Kansas. For more than seven hours of debate, Glenn jabbed and parried, never giving an inch to the Administration's arguments.

All things considered, the final vote was amazingly close. Glenn's resolution of disapproval lost, 48 to 46.

8

The Road to Destruction

Paved with Compromises and Misdirections

The Aftermath

On October 5, the first 19 tons of low-enriched uranium arrived by air in Bombay. But the shipment did little to settle the controversy. As it turned out, all the nuclear cooperation and all the leverage that the State Department insisted would be preserved as a result of this shipment quickly became undone.

While delighted that the White House had won, New Delhi nevertheless warned it would tolerate no further congressional meddling with the second shipment, or a third application for 19.8 tons of uranium, filed the day after the Senate vote.[a]

[a] India applied for a fourth export license for another 19.8 tons on September 1, 1981. These filings followed the schedule the United States had set in 1976. As of this writing, however, neither the 39.6 tons of uranium in the last two applications nor the other 19 tons the Senate approved has been shipped to India.

Several months later, India began to expose the falsity of the State Department's contention that by feeding Tarapur the United States retains leverage to prevent its spent fuel from being reprocessed. The way the Indians now read the fine print of the 1963 agreement, Tarapur's spent fuel can be reprocessed without U.S. permission. A 100-ton-capacity reprocessing plant near Tarapur is now being readied to take the reactor's nuclear waste. As one Indian nuclear industry source told *Nucleonics Week*, a bulletin for the U.S. industry, "It's no longer a question of whether we go ahead and reprocess, but rather when we will get around to it."[1]

Another State Department argument soon evaporated. If Congress disapproves the Tarapur shipments, Warren Christopher had cautioned the Senate Foreign Relations Committee on June 19, "India is very likely to consider itself free of its obligations under the 1963 agreement."[2] Now it appears that after all was said and done and the 38-ton shipment had been approved, both India and the United States want to call it quits on the 1963 agreement.

On February 4, 1981, *The Washington Post* reported that India was trying to wriggle out of the agreement. Recognizing that Tarapur has been a thorn in U.S.-Indian relations, New Delhi suggested it was "amenable to a friendly parting of the ways on the contract," according to *The Post*.

The diplomatic feeler was accompanied by more reprocessing threats. "There is no question of permission from the U.S. for the reprocessing of the Tarapur fuel," Dr. Vvinay N. Meckoni, director of the Tarapur nuclear safety group, told *The Post* during a briefing of foreign journalists. "The fuel belongs to us."[3]

Two months later, the Reagan Administration, anxious to negotiate a termination of the 1963 agreement that still kept safeguards at Tarapur intact, met with Indian officials in Washington to discuss the future of nuclear exports. The Indians were still adamant. They would honor safeguards at Tarapur only if the nuclear shipments were made.[4] A second meeting was held in New Delhi on July 30 and 31, 1981. The State Department wanted assurance that the safeguards would be maintained after the termination as well as a pledge that the Indians would not use U.S. materials for an explosive device. New Delhi still refused to budge. No fuel, no safeguards.[5] On July 29, 1982, the White House finally came up with its solution to the India problem. The French will be allowed to supply Tarapur with nuclear fuel. That way, India gets its uranium and the Nonproliferation Act's restrictions are conveniently sidestepped.

Meanwhile, intelligence reports surfaced that there has been renewed activity at India's Pokharan test site, where its first nuclear bomb was detonated in 1974. No doubt the Indians' renewed interest in "nuclear experiments" has been fueled by the U.S. decision to supply Pakistan with military aid to ward off the presence of Soviet troops in Afghanistan. There have also been reports that Pakistan appears ready to achieve the capability to fabricate a bomb and has begun construction work at a possible test site in the Baluchistan Desert near the Afghan border. The nuclear arms race in Southwest Asia is back in full swing.[6]

The Compromises

A few countries responded favorably to President Carter's decision to defer reprocessing because of their concern over the bomb-making potential of plutonium technologies. But, for the most part, he received a chilly-to-hostile reception overseas. With billions of dollars invested in commercial reprocessing ventures, Britain and France have ignored U.S. appeals to slow down.

Hoping to win the hearts and minds of foreign governments, the Carter Administration gathered together more than forty countries for an International Nuclear Fuel Cycle Evaluation (INFCE) to study alternatives to reprocessing. The maneuver backfired. INFCE endorsed business as usual on the question of recycling plutonium.

Tokyo later lobbied Ronald Reagan to ease restrictions Carter had placed on Japanese reprocessing of U.S.-supplied fuel, and it received blanket permission to reprocess through 1984. Other countries also are expected to pressure for reprocessing.

Carter himself brought on many of the attacks on his nonproliferation policy. The President failed to bury plutonium technology once and for all — first, by conceding, the very day he announced his policy in 1977, that some nations might need reprocessing; and second, by sitting on his hands when allies continued developing and building reprocessing plants.

The Carter reprocessing decision "never had much support in the nuclear bureaucracy," NRC Commissioner Gilinsky lamented in a November 1980 speech. "Our foreign affairs establishment was intimidated by the howls of pain and criticism from our allies and trading partners. Implementation of the policy was diffident, inconsistent, and ultimately unpersuasive, succeeding mainly in convincing others we didn't know what we were doing."[7]

The 1978 Nonproliferation Act took the same beating from the Tarapur vote. While preaching nonproliferation and full-scope safeguards out of one side of its mouth, the Carter Administration pulled out all the stops to supply uranium to the first nation to divert nuclear material for a bomb program. It is hard to imagine how the Administration could have done a better job of undermining a nonproliferation policy.

Where does the Nonproliferation Act now stand? The act requires the United States to renegotiate the agreements for nuclear cooperation it has with more than twenty-five nations to have them comply with the stricter regulations. So far, however, only a handful of agreements have been renegotiated. Yet to be renegotiated are the agreements with key nuclear countries – such as Brazil, Japan, South Africa, and Taiwan – and Euratom, the multinational European atomic community.

The Misdirections

Governments have a habit of hoping for one goal while implementing policies that achieve just the opposite. This has been the case with U.S. nonproliferation policy. Our goal in 1949 was never again to allow nuclear destruction to be unleashed as it was at Hiroshima and Nagasaki. Our policy has been to spread the technology for this terror.

Nuclear weapons-potential technology has been widely disseminated. Teenagers can thumb through library books for enough information to design an atomic bomb. But the technology and equipment was not let out by an invisible hand. It was not spread to the far corners of the earth by some supernatural force. The Iraqis, Pakistanis, Indians, Israelis, and South Africans did not just wake up one morning to find research reactors in their midst. U.S. and foreign government policies are the offending hands. Government policies got us into this mess.

From the beginning, government promotion dominated government control of this source of energy. Nuclear power appeared too lucrative an industrial resource for anyone to heed David Lilienthal's warning in 1946 that "the development of atomic energy for peaceful purposes and the development of atomic energy for bombs are in much of their course interchangeable and interdependent."[8]

People paid more attention to men like T. Keith Glennan, president of Cleveland's Case Institute of Technology, who told the Manufacturing Chemists' Association in a 1952 speech:

Industry built the atomic-energy program; industry carries on nearly all of the work today under government contract; and industry stands ready to utilize the peaceful results of atomic research in its own operations and for the benefit of society. I think it is entirely fair to say that no one has a greater interest in atomic energy than industry.[9]

Indeed, no one had. Eisenhower's Atoms for Peace program made industry its ambassador-at-large for nuclear power and non-proliferation. By 1973, U.S. nuclear companies monopolized the world export market, capturing 86 percent of it for the previous three years. Nuclear power plants have offered a bonanza of export opportunities for American industry. A single 900-megawatt plant commands a price tag well over $1 billion overseas, not to mention almost 20,000 man-years of employment to put it into operation.

All the while, the true commercial value of nuclear power has been hidden by government subsidies and bogus cost esti mates. In addition to almost $40 billion the U.S. government has doled out to its nuclear industry, the Export-Import Bank of the United States has provided $7.2 billion in cheap loans and financial guarantees to build forty-nine nuclear power plants overseas.

With government looking the other way, industry has glossed over the massive auxiliary demands of a nuclear power plant – uranium supply and enrichment, operational safety and maintenance systems, spent fuel storage and final disposal – and marketed just the value of the highly efficient reactor.

"It was as though a fleet of modern jet aircraft, such as Boeing 747s, had been sold to some less-developed country, with the aircrafts and engines working perfectly," according to the Harvard Energy Report. "But to become operational, the fleet obviously would require the support of a sophisticated group of ancillary operations and services, such as airports, air traffic control, and a skilled crew."[10]

The atom that filled industry's coffers did the same for the U.S. foreign policy establishment. Nuclear reactor exports represented one of the largest commercial transactions one country could make with another; it was inevitable the business of the atom would become the business of diplomacy. Not only did nuclear power become a major diplomatic tool for the State Department and other foreign ministries; it became a badge of national honor.

France is "stronger and prouder," Charles de Gaulle grandly declared the day it detonated its first nuclear device in 1960.[11]

"Prediction: Britain will beat the United States in building the first atom plant to supply commercial power to industry," *The Wall Street Journal* admonished in 1952.[12]

Civilian nuclear reactors even became vital components of national security objectives. The first British power plant was advertised as a dual-purpose facility, producing electricity for industry and plutonium for bombs. Uranium helped fuel the Cold War of the 1950s and 1960s.

"If it is possible to develop the peacetime use of atomic energy as a heat source for industrial purposes, it may give us one of the best means of combating the spread of communist influence over the other parts of the world," Walker L. Cisler, president of Detroit-Edison Company, claimed in 1952.[13]

The foot race continues to this day. If Edlow International Company does not ship thirty-eight tons of uranium to Tarapur, the Soviet Ministry of Electric Power will.[b]

Nurturing the industrial-diplomatic pilgrimage has been the delusion that international controls the United States and fellow exporters established would keep all this nuclear harvesting from getting out of hand. Documents like the Nonproliferation Treaty were expected to insure that the peaceful atom never becomes warlike.

Congress, it turns out, has been a willing participant in the hoax. The fairy tale ends with the claim that if ever a country diverts nuclear material, the supplier nation will immediately cut off sales. The Tarapur vote offered Congress the opportunity to put this claim into practice, but Congress backed down.

[b]This security argument is a two-way street. A 1980 report by the Federal Emergency Management Agency concludes that nuclear power plants present security problems for the United States in the event of nuclear war. Centralized electrical generating units, such as nuclear plants, "add to the degree of vulnerability of the U.S. energy system because, as enemy targets, they are larger and there are fewer of them," the report states.

Nuclear Politics Reagan Style

9

The Israeli Raid on Osirak

A Reactor is Destroyed and Once Again the Safeguards Myth is Exposed

The Raid

Eight months after the Tarapur vote, on a late Sunday afternoon, fourteen American-built F-16 fighter-bombers and F-15 interceptors manned by Israeli Air Force pilots raced across northern Saudi Arabia toward Iraq. Their mission: to destroy an Iraqi nuclear reactor being built about twelve miles southeast of Baghdad. The 70-megawatt research reactor, Tamuz I, or as it later became known to the world, Osirak, was a nuclear bomb factory in the view of the Israelis – and in the view of many intelligence experts.

Iraq's public pronouncement that Osirak was a peaceful research reactor, being built to help the country meet future energy demand with nuclear power, was a hoax. Iraq is sitting on thirty billion barrels of oil – more than the United States possesses – and had no energy need for Osirak. The Soviets had already provided Baghdad with a small research reactor fourteen years ago, and Osirak was a much bigger reactor than Iraq required for research. No, Iraq wanted Osirak as part of a long-range plan to build the bomb.

Initially, Iraq went to the Soviet Union for the large research reactor it wanted. But the Soviets, long skittish about nonweapons states possessing nuclear weapons-potential technology, turned them down. So the Iraqis turned to France, which, besides having had no qualms about selling nuclear merchandise, depended on Iraq for about one-fifth of its oil imports.

The research reactor France agreed to build for Iraq was one of the most advanced that Paris had to offer. It consisted of a core of reactor fuel suspended in a tank of water – a particularly good setup for making bombs. The core had open spaces where specimens would be inserted for irradiation tests. But with some minor modifications in the pipework, cooling system, and racks – all of which would take no more than a few weeks to complete – the open spaces could be adapted to hold natural uranium. The natural uranium – of which Iraq had already bought several hundred tons – could then be irradiated to produce plutonium.

Even more disturbing is the fact that the French supplied Iraq with eighty kilograms of highly enriched uranium, whose U-235 content had been increased to the bomb-grade 93 percent level. With the right technology and know-how Iraq might divert this fuel and have a weapon fabricated in six months.

The French were not the only ones the Iraqis tapped. The Italians – starved for nuclear business and just as dependent on Iraq for oil as were the French – agreed to equip the Osirak research facility with specially shielded labs to handle radioactive materials. The labs, called "hot cells," would enable Iraq to reprocess spent fuel from the research reactor to extract its plutonium. The labs thus further shortened the distance Iraq had to travel to reach the bomb.

Estimates of just how close Iraq actually was to acquiring nuclear weapons range from several years to the end of the decade. As far as Israel was concerned, however close Iraq was to the bomb was much too close. Galling for the Israelis was the fact that Iraq was marching toward the bomb while observing all the nonproliferation rules and safeguards the world community had established, ostensibly to prevent such a thing from happening. Baghdad was an early signer of the 1970 Nonproliferation Treaty and had agreed to accept IAEA safeguards at Osirak.

No matter. In Menachem Begin's eyes, nuclear weapons in the hands of Iraq could never be tolerated and if the world community would not or could not do anything about it, Israel would. In this case, the Israeli Air Force would do the job. On June 7, 1981, the fourteen Israeli F-16s and F-15s swooped down upon Osirak and with precision bombing reduced the reactor to a pile of rubble.

World reaction to the attack was swift and harsh. The French claimed that the attack only complicated an already explosive situation. Arab nations, many of whom were privately breathing a sigh of relief that Iraq's nuclear weapons program had been set back, nevertheless united to condemn Israel. The Soviets accused the United States of conspiring with the Israelis in launching the raid. The U.N. Security Council voted unanimously to condemn Israel for the bombing. The United States criticized the Israeli raid, suspended arms shipments temporarily, then let the issue die. Saddam Hussein let his true colors show after the raid by calling on other nations to "help the Arabs in one way or another to acquire atomic bombs."[1]

Particularly offended was the agency whose responsibility it was to ensure that material at Osirak was not diverted for a bomb – the Vienna-based International Atomic Energy Agency. According to IAEA officials, the Israelis had acted like vigilantes taking international law into their own hands. The agency voted at its General Conference three months later to suspend any technical help to Israel. It also called on other member states to stop supplying Israel with nuclear materials and technology. Sigvard Eklund, then the director of IAEA, fumed, "From a point of principle, one can only conclude that it is the agency's safeguards system that has been attacked."[2]

Dr. Eklund was certainly correct. But the Israelis were not the only ones attacking. The IAEA and the safeguards system it implements have long been under fire. And the Israeli raid on Iraq, a raid on a nation under the best nuclear controls the world offers, merely pointed out again that the safeguards system the international community has set up to prevent diversions is terribly flawed.

The IAEA

Many of the world's nuclear facilities, other than those in the nuclear-weapons states, are under IAEA safeguards. The safeguards are set up to ensure that the member nations comply with the 1970 Nonproliferation Treaty – that is, that their nuclear programs are peaceful and that no nuclear materials are being diverted for nuclear explosives or other military purposes. The individual countries voluntarily conclude safeguard agreements with the IAEA.

Save for curtailment of IAEA assistance or suspension of membership privileges, the agency has few sanctions it can levy on a state if it uncovers diversion. About the most it can do is sound the alarm that it has detected diversion and let the international community take action. Also, the IAEA concerns itself only with possible diversion *by* the state, not diversion *from* the state. The member nations are responsible for making sure that terrorists or criminals do not get their hands on nuclear materials. The agency keeps an eye on the nations.

The IAEA attempts to set up its safeguards agreements with member nations so that the agency can detect in a timely manner diversion of "significant quantities" of nuclear material.[3] To do this, the agency's Safeguards Department can take various surveillance and containment measures, such as installing tamper-resistant automatic cameras at nuclear facilities or placing seals on fuel containers between inspections.

A good deal of the agency's safeguards work is done through inspections, which consist of an accounting and verification system based on reports submitted by the nation's nuclear facilities. The nuclear plant operator, for example, keeps records on nuclear materials at the facility. The IAEA then reviews these records to make sure all the material is accounted for. The agency supplements its review with visits to the facility, during which IAEA inspectors will actually count or measure nuclear material and compare it to what has been reported by the plant operator. So far, the IAEA reports that it knows of no safeguarded items that have been diverted.

The Safeguards Myth

While on paper the IAEA safeguards may appear adequate, in reality they are not. The international inspections system, it turns out, has glaring weaknesses, which undermine the very belief that the peaceful atom can be both promoted and kept peaceful.

As noted before, while 115 nations subscribe to full-scope IAEA safeguards, 48 nations do not because they have not signed the 1970 Nonproliferation Treaty. The nonsignatories include nations believed to be clandestinely building bombs, such as India, Pakistan, South Africa, and Israel.

In addition, the countries that have signed the treaty are allowed to back out of it at any time. This makes signing and accepting safeguards in many ways an attractive option for countries intent on building a bomb. Iraq, for example, is able to collect all the nuclear materials and technology needed to build the bomb, all done under IAEA safeguards. Once Iraq is ready to fabricate a weapon, it only has to give three months notice and it can withdraw from the treaty and the IAEA inspectors are off its soil.

Also, while the treaty prohibits a nonweapons state from acquiring or manufacturing "nuclear weapons," it is vague about whether a country can take all the necessary steps short of building a bomb, such as designing or testing its non-nuclear components.

There are also numerous problems with the safeguards themselves:

Conflict of Interest

The IAEA has two responsibilities: (1) to promote and (2) to safeguard nuclear power. The agency, however, has been more concerned with the former than the latter. The question arises: Can an agency both promote an enterprise and regulate it? Many believe it cannot. "There is an inherent conflict of interest between promoting and regulating civilian nuclear power activities, noted Democratic Senator Gary Hart of Colorado. "In this country, it led to the establishment of the independent Nuclear Regulatory Commission to replace the Atomic Energy Commission."[4]

Inspections and Accounting Weaknesses

The IAEA's some 140 inspectors have been criticized as being poorly trained and spread too thin for the 700 nuclear reactors and related facilities around the world under safeguards.

The agency's accounting methods, which are being used to keep track of nuclear fuel, have also been criticized for being too loose and too dependent on host-country figures. The problem is due partly to the nature of the material being accounted for. During chemical reprocessing, for example, measurement limitations and weight variations can cause up to 1 percent out of every 220 pounds of material to be unavoidably unaccounted for.

The IAEA detection standards, however, are also established out of political compromise so as to be as unobtrusive as possible for the host country. For example, the annual detection threshold the agency has set (this is the amount of material the IAEA will allow to be classified as unavoidably unaccounted for in a country before it suspects diversion) is about eighteen pounds of plutonium – enough to fuel one explosive device. The IAEA standards, in effect, have a margin of error of about one bomb per year.

The Secrecy

Worse still, no one outside of the agency knows whether these detection standards and safeguards actually work. To insure that industrial secrets will not be leaked to other nations, IAEA inspection agreements with host countries and the results of those inspections are kept confidential. "In our opinion," concluded a 1976 General Accounting Office report, "the United States does not possess sufficient information to judge the adequacy of the current IAEA system."[5]

The U.S. NRC further warned in November 1981 that it was "concerned that the IAEA safeguards system would not detect a diversion in at least some types of facilities. In addition," it said, "we are not confident that the member states would be notified of a diversion in a timely fashion."[6]

Deception and Loopholes

The IAEA's inspection and auditing procedures vary so much from country to country and are so riddled with loopholes, that the host nation would have little difficulty deceiving an inspector. A 1976 report by Barber Associates, prepared for the U.S. Energy Research and Development Administration, shows how the deception might come about:

> In the case of a suspected diversion by a national government the response to such an accusation would be extremely difficult. It is unlikely that an international inspector will ever witness a diversion; all he will have to go on will be indirect evidence – discrepancies between the suspect nation's domestic accounting system and the audit of the international inspectorate, breakdown in remote observation equipment, or suspicious procedural roadblocks in the way of international inspection. The nation involved could argue that such discrepancies were due to human error, mechanical failure, or normal process loss – and it could well be correct. In such an uncertain atmosphere, the IAEA would be very hesitant in making public accusations.[7]

One of the best real-life examples of the deception and loopholes comes from Iraq. On June 19, 1981, about two weeks after the Israeli bombing of Osirak, Roger Richter, an American inspector with the IAEA who was assigned to the Middle East section that dealt with Iraq, testified before the Senate Foreign Relations Committee.

Richter, who resigned from the IAEA about a week after the Israeli bombing, was the only American assigned to Iraq. Since 1976, the other inspectors have come from the Soviet Union or Hungary, two of Iraq's allies.

"Countries have a right to veto inspectors from whatever countries they choose, a right they regularly exercise," Richter pointed out to the committee. "As an accepted inspector, you must keep in mind that any adverse conclusions you might reach as a result of your inspections would have to take into account your country's sensitivity to how this information might affect relations with Iraq."

Iraq was always given several weeks notice of a planned inspection, more than enough time to hide any secret activity. Also, under the agreement the IAEA had with Iraq, the agency was "limited to only three inspections per year," Richter testified, "usually spaced at approximately four-month intervals. Since the entire reactor can be emptied of the clandestine uranium target specimens within days, you as an inspector face the fact that by the time you arrive to verify the declared inventory of fuel elements, which power the reactor, all evidence of illicit irradiations could be covered up."

Furthermore, loopholes in the IAEA inspection agreement enabled a number of critical items at Osirak to be exempted from agency safeguards – such as the pilot reprocessing facility, fuel fabrication equipment, and *100 tons* of uranium oxide.

The IAEA inspector spends most of his inspection time looking over accounting papers put in front of him by the plant operators. "The difficult part of the job is that you must prepare yourself mentally to ignore the many signs that may indicate the presence of clandestine activities going on in the facilities adjacent to the reactor," Richter said. "You will now complete a standard report, filling in the blanks. You will try to forget that you have just been party to a very misleading process."[8]

The Goodwill Factor

In the end, IAEA inspectors depend on the goodwill of the host country. But even that sometimes is missing. For example, on September 30, 1980, eight months before the Israeli bombing, two

Phantom jets that bore the markings of the Iranian Air Force (some suspected they were Israeli jets in disguise) attacked Osirak, slightly damaging the facility. IAEA inspectors were temporarily barred for about two months from entering Iraq to check the secret whereabouts of twenty-six pounds of highly enriched uranium the French had supplied.

The Paper Tiger

Even if diversion is detected, the international community in the past has been loathe to do anything about it. India is the best example. The United States only disapproved of India's 1974 explosion; it did not stop shipping uranium. And, in the face of further refusals to accept international safeguards or to renounce nuclear explosions, the Executive Branch went out of its way to again feed an Indian reactor.

The manifold weaknesses of the IAEA point to only one conclusion: The international safeguards system that the world has established to prevent the spread of nuclear weapons sits atop a house of cards.

The 1970 Nonproliferation Treaty, which 115 nations have signed, depends on an inspections and control system that will not stop the spread of nuclear weapons. Furthermore, the 1978 U.S. Nonproliferation Act rests upon the same inadequate control system. The 1978 act requires that countries that have not signed the 1970 international treaty adopt full-scope IAEA safeguards before the United States will supply them nuclear materials. The countries must place all their nuclear facilities under the IAEA inspections and control system, as if they were signatories of the 1970 treaty. But even full-scope safeguards are inadequate. Even if India had agreed to safeguards and the United States had shipped all the fuel, the problem of proliferation would have remained. As Iraq has demonstrated, the presence of IAEA inspectors in a country does not prevent it from building a bomb.

The Reagan Administration, however, would have the world believe otherwise. That is because Ronald Reagan has big plans for worldwide nuclear power. And those plans include maintaining the charade that the IAEA will remain a policeman of nuclear power.

10

The Reagan
Nuclear Policy
A Recipe for
Destruction

F or all the rebuffs from our trading partners, for all the debilitating effects of industry opposition, all the undercutting by the State Department, all the hedging, flip-flopping, and poor administration from the Oval Office, the Carter years may have provided the only daylight nonproliferation will see.

Ronald Reagan, the candidate who, when asked if the United States should oppose nuclear proliferation, responded, "I just don't think it's any of our business," appears to be abiding by that statement as president.[1]

At Home

The U.S. nuclear industry, which in the past decade has seen its domestic market collapse and its foreign sales slip to European competitors, has been giddy with excitement over prospects of a four-year Christmas with the Reagan Administration.

Under the stewardship of James B. Edwards, former South Carolina governor and strong supporter of the now-idle Barnwell reprocessing plant in his state, the Department of Energy has kicked conservation and solar power funding into the streets to fend for itself in the marketplace. The Department of Energy's Fiscal Year 1982 appropriation for solar energy and other renewables was $376 million, almost half what it was in FY 1981. The Reagan Administration wants to cut it further in FY 1983 – to $83 million, which would represent a 78 percent decrease. Conservation has fared even worse. Its FY 1982 appropriation of $386 million, down $245 million from FY 1981, would be slashed 94 percent in FY 1983 to $21.8 million.

Meanwhile, the nuclear industry continues to be presented welfare checks that would make Adam Smith turn over in his grave. While Jimmy Carter viewed nuclear power as an energy source of last resort, Ronald Reagan sees it as a substantial contributor to the nation's energy needs. All told, 87 percent of the Department of Energy's FY 1983 budget for energy technologies would go to nuclear programs. The Administration also is pushing for a speedup of the nuclear regulatory process so the industry can have its plants operating sooner. Clinch River, the Tennessee breeder reactor project that President Carter tried to terminate, and whose federal subsidy Reagan's own budget director, David Stockman, criticized as running against the free-market grain, has been ordered completed. The project is budgeted for $252 million in FY 1983, an increase of $59 million over the previous year. And if all this were not enough, the nuclear industry has asked the Reagan Administration for a $50 billion bailout to support its dying business.

Just as disturbing is the Reagan proposal to dismantle the Department of Energy and parcel out its duties to several other departments. At home, dismemberment would cripple the federal government's ability to deal with energy supply emergencies, weaken its capacity to coordinate national energy policy, and destroy the partnership that has developed between the national and state governments over energy matters. Abroad, dismemberment would send a clear message that the United States is no longer committed to solving its energy problems.

Overseas

It is overseas that nuclear politics Ronald Reagan style poses the greatest danger. In place of the Ford-Carter policy to restrict commerce in sensitive nuclear technologies, such as reprocessing, the Reagan Administration appears eager to implement a nuclear renaissance that gives scant attention to its proliferation hazards.

The Reliable Supplier

While the Ford and Carter Administrations attempted to make the United States a *responsible* nuclear supplier, the Reagan Administration appears intent on making us a *reliable* supplier. "The United States will cooperate with other nations in the peaceful uses of nuclear energy, including civil nuclear programs to meet their energy security needs, under a regime of adequate safeguards and controls," President Reagan explained at a July 16, 1981, press conference. "This is essential to our nonproliferation goals. If we are not such a partner, other countries will tend to go their own ways and our influence will diminish."[2]

The Reagan policy thus appears to be nothing more than a warmed-over version of Atoms for Peace. Nuclear power again will become a diplomatic tool to be manipulated in the context of overall U.S. security requirements. In other words, the United States will return to a policy of selective proliferation for countries that the White House concludes pose no threat, and nonproliferation for countries that do.

To grease the skids for this reliable supply initiative, the Administration wants to speed up Executive Branch approval on nuclear export requests. The State Department has already floated proposals to eliminate what clout the 1978 Nonproliferation Act had left after Tarapur and to consolidate nuclear export control under its wing. On the hit list, for example, is the NRC, the first agency to stand in the way of the State Department's plans to ship uranium to India. Among the proposals being considered at State is one to transfer export licensing authority from the NRC to the State Department. That way, the NRC would never again interfere in the State Department's plans to employ nuclear diplomacy.

In order to avoid any more nasty fights like Tarapur, the State Department also has proposed that the Nonproliferation Act be rewritten to remove the retroactive application of new conditions, such as the full-scope safeguards requirement, on old nuclear export agreements. The United States thus would be able to continue nuclear cooperation with countries like India, South Africa, Brazil, and Argentina, regardless of whether they have accepted full-scope safeguards.

The Reagan Administration also plans to carry gifts of nuclear hardware in one hand and conventional weapons in the other. The White House argues that supplying more conventional arms to some countries, as it proposes to do with Pakistan, will reduce their "motivation" to acquire nuclear weapons.[3] Pakistan, however, is the best example of a country that will accept the conventional arms and still pursue the nuclear option. Indeed, it appears that rather than dissuading some countries from acquiring nuclear weapons, a conventional arms buildup only makes them more interested in going nuclear—as the conventional arms buildup in the Middle East is beginning to demonstrate.

Arms control analyst Steven J. Baker writes:

> In the Middle East and Persian Gulf, conventional arms transfers have helped to create large, effective military establishments with a dominant claim on the resources of their nations. Trained by the great powers and schooled in the military dogmas of the great powers, these military establishments are likely to see nuclear weapons as a complement to the nuclear-capable delivery systems which they are importing at an increasingly fast rate.[4]

Atoms For War

A dangerous shift the Reagan Administration has made in U.S. nonproliferation policy has been its decision to junk the previous administration's restrictions on reprocessing. Reagan also announced on July 16 that, from now on, the United States would "not inhibit or set back civil reprocessing and breeder reactor development abroad in nations with advanced nuclear programs where it does not constitute a proliferation risk." At the same time, the White House proposed to beef up the IAEA to insure that the plutonium coming from reprocessing and breeders is not diverted to nuclear weapons.[5] A year later the Administration was ready to give some preferred nations receiving U.S. nuclear fuel "blanket approval" to reprocess spent fuel.[6]

Lifting restrictions on commercial reprocessing, however, will only help shorten the path nonweapons states must take to acquire weapons-grade plutonium. Approving reprocessing for other nations also will leave the United States with little credibility in persuading countries it believes are proliferation risks to forego this technology.

Furthermore, relying on the IAEA to insure that a reprocessing revival does not get out of hand only adds to the charade that the danger of increased plutonium production can be contained. The fact is, while the IAEA's ability to safeguard all nuclear facilities may be subject to debate, its ability to safeguard plutonium in reprocessing plants is not. The almost unanimous conclusion among nuclear experts is that the agency cannot safeguard plutonium, which has left the Defense Department, for one, concerned that the White House is relying too much on the IAEA.

The problem of plutonium and safeguards was summed up best in a 1982 speech by former NRC Commissioner Peter Bradford before the Public Citizen forum: "Separated plutonium is directly usable in a bomb. A nation with a designed and fabricated weapon could fuel it with diverted plutonium in less time than detecting and reporting the diversion might take. I know of no one knowledgeable about safeguards who disputes this. Thus, the convergence of President Reagan's policies toward reprocessing and breeder reactors with the problems in IAEA safeguards . . . threatens to overwhelm the international safeguards system altogether. Large quantities of separate plutonium being transported, stored, and fabricated cannot be adequately safeguarded."[7]

The White House's decision to open the reprocessing market has been alarming. What has been downright frightening is the trial balloon the Administration has floated on fabricating nuclear weapons from the spent fuel of civilian reactors. In a move that alarmed even some nuclear industry executives, President Reagan has directed Energy Secretary Edwards to study "the feasibility of obtaining economical plutonium supplies for the Department of Energy by means of a competitive procurement."[5] The Energy Department, which builds the nuclear warheads for the Department of Defense, has been worried that government reactors will not be able to produce enough plutonium to make the 17,000 bombs the White House wants to build over the next fifteen years. The spent fuel from civilian reactors, such as Three Mile Island or Indian Point, would be reprocessed to extract the plutonium, which would be purified for bomb-making purposes by laser isotope separation. Proponents of the idea argue that building nuclear weapons from civilian spent fuel thus would save the government billions of dollars otherwise spent on new facilities to produce plutonium.

Building nuclear weapons from the spent fuel also would turn civilian reactors into bomb factories. Overnight, the separation that has been maintained over the past two decades between civilian reactors and the military would no longer exist. Paul Leventhal, president of the nonproliferation group Nuclear Control – Citizens to Stop the Spread of Nuclear Arms, put the consequences in stark terms before a March 1982 hearing of my Oversight and Investigations Subcommittee: "Any move by the federal government to use commercial nuclear power spent fuel for making nuclear weapons would break down the final barrier between atoms for peace and atoms for war. It would set a dangerous example for other nations to follow. It would render meaningless efforts by the United States to dissuade foreign governments from using their commercial nuclear facilities to provide a weapons option. Ultimately, it would lead to a world awash in plutonium and bedeviled by nuclear violence."[8]

How successful Reagan will be in loosening nonproliferation restrictions remains to be seen. The proposal to mine civilian reactors for bomb fuel has met stiff opposition in Congress. The Senate already has passed a two-year moratorium on such a move. Any attempt to gut the Nonproliferation Act and slip the export licensing authority out of the NRC's back door also will run into resistance on Capitol Hill. While a 1981 Government Accounting Office report suggested that the export licensing process could be more timely and predictable, it recommended, nonetheless, that licensing authority remain with the NRC. And though the Reagan Administration has pledged to make the United States once again a reliable supplier, the general consensus in and out of the industry is that the nuclear market is so depressed at the moment there are very few foreign customers for the supplies.

Nevertheless, the direction of the Reagan nuclear policy overseas seems clear. The Carter experiment with nuclear detoxification will not be pursued. Nonproliferation will no longer stand in the way of a good State Department deal. While the worldwide nuclear market is shrinking, the half dozen or so nonweapons states that have set out to develop nuclear weapons – countries like India, Pakistan, South Africa, and Argentina – are still eager nuclear customers. The United States, however, will play a significantly reduced role in trying to restrain their access to nuclear material. Ronald Reagan appears determined to return the United States to the European fold, whose policy is that suppliers control the spread of nuclear weapons by a vigorous commercial presence overseas.

The nuclear reactor salesmen are back on the road.

11

Vertical Proliferation
Arming for the Last War While Starting the Next War

Less than a week after President Carter signed the 1978 Nonproliferation Act, the United States set off another underground nuclear device at a southern Nevada test range. The explosion was one of a dozen this country conducted that year. The same year, the Soviet Union conducted more than two dozen.

The numbers do not go unnoticed. For more than thirty-five years the superpowers have lectured the nonweapons states on the dangers of acquiring nuclear arms, and for more than thirty-five years the United States and Soviet Union have mass produced nuclear weapons. India was scorned by the weapons states for detonating one nuclear device. So far, the five other members of the nuclear club have conducted about thirteen hundred nuclear test explosions.

In Article VI of the 1970 Nonproliferation Treaty, the weapons states pledged to halt the arms race and to begin reducing their arsenals. But three decades and sixteen international treaties after the first atomic bomb incinerated Hiroshima, the superpowers have made only a token effort to curb their appetite for more nuclear weapons. In the final analysis, the superpowers' arms race has been constrained only by cost and technological limitations. Otherwise, the motto on both sides has been: "If it can be built, build it, and worry about the arms race another day."

The resulting overkill has been mindboggling. The weapons states now have more than 50,000 nuclear warheads with a total explosive power equal to one million Hiroshima bombs. One Poseidon submarine has enough nuclear firepower to cause 30 million fatalities in the Soviet Union – more than it suffered in all of World War II. In Europe alone, the United States has a nuclear weapon for every fifty American soldiers.[1] Just 200 of the 9,000 strategic warheads in the U.S. arsenal would destroy every major city in the Soviet Union.

The disregard that both the United States and the Soviet Union have shown toward nuclear disarmament has left them with little credibility to persuade other nations to renounce nuclear arms. While administration after administration has blamed the arms race on Soviet belligerence, the fact is that both sides are at fault. Both sides have served as models for a nuclear arms race among nonweapons states.

The Arms Racers

While the stated policy of the superpowers has been to deter nuclear war, the armaments they have developed have brought the world closer to war. Rather than ease tension and achieve stability, Moscow and Washington have allowed themselves to be caught up in a nuclear weapons spiral that has increased the pressure on both sides to empty their silos in a crisis. While both sides have professed that their awesome capacity for destruction has no military utility because no sane person would ever push the button, both sides are building weapons, like the Soviet SS-18 and the American MX missiles which are used to start nuclear wars not deter them.

Arming for MAD

Initially, there was a surge of concern over the horrors of nuclear war. With Hiroshima and Nagasaki fresh in their minds, President Truman and other Western leaders called for the renunciation of nuclear weapons. But the disarmament fever soon faded. Distrust between the United States and the Soviet Union was growing, and the Cold War was heating up. Soon, all thoughts of stopping an arms race before it ever started were shelved as both sides attempted to one-up the other in weapons development.

Five years after the United States exploded the atomic bomb, the Soviets exploded theirs in 1949. By 1955, the United States had jet intercontinental bombers. The Soviets soon had theirs. In 1957, the Soviets successfully flight-tested an intercontinental ballistic missile (ICBM). The United States tested its ICBM a year later, and by 1962 both sides had missiles that could reach the other's homeland with up to a 10-megaton payload.

In 1957, the Soviets orbited Sputnik I. The space race had begun and Americans worried over a missile gap. In 1958, the United States had a satellite in orbit. By 1960, the United States had its first nuclear-powered submarine that could fire ballistic missiles. The Soviets had a comparable sub by 1968. In 1970, the United States began deploying multiple independently targetable reentry vehicles (MIRVs). MIRVed missiles carry several warheads, each of which can be aimed at a different target. Five years later, the Soviets began deploying MIRVs.

By the end of the 1960s, the Soviets had built up enough of a retaliatory capacity that, for all intents and purposes, a parity existed between the superpowers' nuclear arsenals. Both sides could insure that a nuclear conflict would result in both countries being effectively destroyed.

The United States and the Soviet Union had thus formed a suicide pact, and it was this pact, oddly enough, that kept both countries alive. The superpowers' leaders would be deterred from launching their missiles because to do so would result in "mutual assured destruction." (The scenario was appropriately acronymed MAD.) While the civilian population was justifiably uneasy about being held hostage to nuclear weapons, the fact of the matter was that the world had indeed gone mad and the only sane deterrence to nuclear war was the recognition, and, yes, the assurance, that any nuclear exchange would be the last.

By the early 1960s, another approach to deal with certain aspects of the arms race had come into place: arms control. Under arms control, the United States and the Soviet Union would negotiate treaties that attempted to manage the dangers and costs of a nuclear arms race, to limit the damage if a nuclear conflict did break out, and to reduce the chances of nuclear war occurring.

Accordingly, in 1963 (a year after the Cuban missile crisis) a Washington-Moscow hotline was established and the Limited Test Ban Treaty was signed. A treaty prohibiting nuclear weapons in Latin America was completed in 1967, followed by the Nonproliferation Treaty. Nuclear weapons were banned in outer space and on the seabed and agreements were signed to reduce the risk of accidental war. While all the early arms control agreements were steps in the right direction, it must be remembered that in many cases they prohibited weapons deployments that the two superpowers had no intention of undertaking in the first place. The Strategic Arms Limitation Talks of the 1970s marked the first attempt by the United States and the Soviet Union to deal with the strategic weaponry they had in place or planned to deploy. With SALT, the superpowers made the first step toward living up to their end of the bargain with the Nonproliferation Treaty – that is, to stop the arms race and begin nuclear disarmament.

The talks produced a 1972 SALT I Interim Agreement and Protocol that set caps on submarine-launched ballistic missiles and ICBMS until a more comprehensive agreement could be reached. The talks also produced the Anti-Ballistic Missile (ABM) Treaty, which, when its protocol was agreed to, limited both sides to two ballistic missile sites each. The ABM Treaty was noteworthy because it marked the one and only time the superpowers have agreed not to pursue a strategic weapons system they had planned to build. It should be noted, however, that the primary motivation behind foregoing ABMs was the fact that neither side had the technology then to build them.

After seven years of negotiations, Jimmy Carter and Leonid Brezhnev signed SALT II in 1979. SALT II placed ceilings on many strategic launchers, as well as subceilings on different types of specific missiles, such as MIRVed missiles. The treaty also attempted to restrain further modernization of the strategic forces on both sides and to serve as a starting point for future reductions.

SALT II's fate is well known. Liberals criticized the treaty because its ceilings were too high. Conservatives, led by Ronald Reagan's presidential campaign, savaged it because they claimed it gave the Soviets unfair numerical advantages in certain weapons. The Russians then effectively killed SALT II with their brutal invasion of Afghanistan in December 1979. President Carter gave up, and Senate ratification of the treaty was deferred indefinitely.

Though the Reagan Administration has pledged to abide by its provisions as long as the Soviet Union does, the demise of SALT II as a treaty was a tragic loss. Without it, Soviet strategic forces may eventually increase higher than the treaty's limits. SALT I and II also moved the superpowers in the direction of achieving strategic stability and of fulfilling this country's obligation under the Nonproliferation Treaty.

Even so, SALT and the previous arms control agreements should not be viewed through rose-colored glasses. After all, they made only small advances toward solving the problem of vertical proliferation, for even with their restrictions, the treaties and agreements have still allowed both superpowers to amass huge stockpiles of nuclear weapons.

Writes William H. Kincaid, director of the Arms Control Association:

> The significance, or insignificance, of strategic arms limitation to date cannot adequately be judged without an appreciation of parallel trends in weapons development. Throughout the period under discussion, of course, both superpowers have maintained robust production and research and development programs. . . . While pursuing a basically (or at least nominally) deterrent doctrine, the U.S. has never forsworn any technologically feasible innovation that would add to the so-called warfighting ability of its forces, should deterrence fail. It has pioneered the development of rapid retargeting systems; smaller, higher yield warheads; multiple warheads; evasive warheads; improved guidance systems; modern cruise missiles; tactical and theatre nuclear weapons; and penetration aids – all of which contribute to the flexibility and warfighting potential of its forces. Indeed, it is quite fair to say that the particular elaboration or extension of deterrence theory in any era has been chiefly determined by technological opportunities and constraints, *not* by holy writ.
>
> In none of these developments has the Soviet Union shown the way. Yet in none of these developments is the Soviet Union barred from approximating the U.S. capability. And the experience of the last 15 years or more suggests that it will bend every effort to do so. Moreover, the U.S.S.R. has over this period developed its own vigorous production and technology base, giving it a deployment potential which would severely tax U.S. resources to match, if it became necessary. . . .
>
> Overall, the trend over the last 30 years in the development of strategic weapons has been consistently in the direction of exploiting technology to introduce new systems while constantly improving existing delivery vehicles and nuclear explosives. The result is a proliferation of hedges against anticipated threats but also a diversification and proliferation of threats.[2]

While institutional inertia and unavoidable technological progress have fueled the arms race, there is still plenty of blame left over for the political leaders of the superpowers. Although the United States has continually renounced the use of nuclear weapons, there have been few international crises or conflicts where its public officials have not either privately considered or discreetly threatened to employ them (the Berlin crisis and Korean War being the most notable examples). On the other side, the Soviet Union's massive arms buildup in the past 15 years and its interventions in Angola, Ethiopia, Cambodia, Afghanistan, and Poland have done nothing but undercut strategic arms negotiations.

While both superpowers have pledged their commitment to deter nuclear war, both are now producing or attempting to produce missiles that are designed to be first-strike weapons. In the past, Soviet and American missiles have not been capable of destroying the other's missiles that are housed in underground silos. Each side could thus absorb a first strike and be assured of having its land-based missiles survive to fire in retaliation. But the Soviet Union and the United States have developed missiles like the SS-18 and MX that are accurate and powerful enough to destroy the other's land-based missiles. They are designed to be fired first in order to disarm a portion of the enemy's nuclear force. These weapons thus reduce each side's retaliatory capacity and increase instability. Herbert Scoville, Jr., president of the Arms Control Association, explains: "The danger is multiplied many times when both nations have a countersilo capability. Then both perceive increased advantage from striking first and disadvantage from allowing the other to launch the first strike." The incentive to strike first is certainly diminished by the fact that if either side did so it would risk devastating retaliation from surviving submarine-launched missiles and bombers. Nonetheless, developing a countersilo capability "is a trend in the wrong direction," Scoville notes. "A very destabilizing situation is created, since in time of acute crisis, such as a large-scale conflict in Europe, the pressure to launch could become almost intolerable." The pressure would also mount for both sides to launch on warning of an attack to avoid losing land-based missiles in a first strike. The launch-on-warning tactic "is extremely dangerous. It would greatly increase the risk that a nuclear conflict could break out by accident. Radars and computers can fail and create false alarms; in this case a false alarm could mean Armageddon."[3]

By the end of the 1970s another dangerous concept came into vogue — that of limited and winnable nuclear war. American presidents have chafed over the fact that under the MAD scenario any use of nuclear weapons would result in mutually assured destruction. It was thus argued that in time of extreme crisis an American president .should have other war fighting options that would allow for the use of nuclear weapons in a limited fashion but would not result in all-out nuclear war and mutual destruction. (The Soviets are assumed to be planning for the same type of conflict.) By the summer of 1980, President Carter had signed a Presidential Directive on strategic nuclear targeting policy (PD-59) that would enable the United States to fire its missiles at selected military targets and supposedly to control the escalation of fighting so it would not result in all-out nuclear war. That way, the United States would be able to fight, survive, and win a nuclear conflict. Nuclear weapons finally would have a military utility. The United States has thus begun developing a nuclear war fighting capability, which rests on the assumption that there will be controlled escalation in a nuclear exchange to keep the world from going MAD.

The assumption, however, has totally abandoned reality. The limited war scenario assumes that once a nuclear exchange begins, both sides' leaders, if they are still alive, can surgically control the damage. It assumes that both sides can endure twenty million deaths in a limited nuclear exchange on Friday, then sit down Saturday and negotiate a ceasefire to keep the remaining missiles from being launched. In other words, it assumes that war can be waged rationally – when history has proven this to be rarely the case – and that nuclear war can be won, when in reality there would be no winners.

The Reagan Administration, however, appears intent on perpetuating the unrealistic assumptions and on moving a step further with talk of a "window of vulnerability."

The Soviet Union is thought by some to be ahead of the United States in countersilo weapons. President Reagan's window of vulnerability theory assumes that in an extreme crisis, like the Cuban missile stand-off, the Soviets might be tempted to launch 200 of their SS-18s, confident that the 2,000 warheads atop those launchers would destroy most of the 1,000 land-based U.S. ICBMs. Other Soviet ICBMs and submarine-launched ballistic missiles also would knock out U.S. stragegic bombers on airfields and submarines in port. An American president would then be left in a quandary. He could accept elimination of his land-based nuclear capacity and the initial casualties. Or he could fire the remaining submarine-launched missiles and invite further devastation from a Soviet counterattack.

But to accept this scenario we must accept more unrealistic assumptions. We must assume that the Soviets could launch a near-perfect attack, which would eliminate with split-second timing our land-based missiles and most of our submarine and bombers not in the air or underwater. Such a simultaneous attack requiring near-perfect accuracy would be almost impossible to pull off. The scenario assumes that if the president allows his land-based missiles to be destroyed and suffers ten to twenty million casualties, he will sit on his hands and not fire any of the 3,000 to 4,000 remaining warheads deployed in invulnerable U.S. submarines on patrol. In other words, it assumes a type of limited nuclear war that will never take place.

The Reagan Administration, nevertheless, has launched a major arms buildup with which to fight this type of war. It is expanding warhead production. It plans to increase the country's capability to strike first by deploying missiles, like the MX on land and the Trident II in submarines, that can knock out Soviet land-based missiles. Dangerous talk has come from the White House, the Defense Department, and the State Department about using nuclear weapons as instruments of foreign and military policy. The Pentagon, under Defense Secretary

Caspar W. Weinberger, has even begun developing strategies for fighting and winning a "protracted" nuclear war with the Soviets. Ridiculous statements are being uttered by Administration officials about nuclear warning shots, limited war in Europe, and civil defense measures to survive a nuclear attack.

The White House, for example, has announced it wants to launch a $4 billion program to relocate two-thirds of the American public in case of a threat of nuclear war. Not only would such a program be a waste of money, it would dangerously lull the public into thinking it can survive a nuclear holocaust and thus win a nuclear war. The fact is that there will be no winners when the bombs explode.

While the Reagan Administration insists, as previous administrations have done, that it is arming to deter war, its rhetoric, its policies, and its weapons are edging the world closer to the brink of war.

The Spectators

Where does the nuclear arms buildup of the superpowers leave the spectators – that is, the nonweapons states that have the capability to build weapons but have not done so? For one, it has left many of them understandably outraged over vertical proliferation. Some of their diplomats have even said that if they had known the superpowers would have so flagrantly ignored the disarmament clause of the Nonproliferation Treaty they would have advised their leaders not to sign the document.

The frustrations of the nonweapons states were made public at the second Review Conference of the Nonproliferation Treaty held in Geneva in 1980. The 1970 treaty mandated that the signers gather every five years to assess the progress both the nonweapons and the weapons states have made in complying with its provisions. The 1975 Review Conference, though contentious, ended with a declaration by the participating nations reaffirming the value of the treaty and their commitment to nonproliferation. The 1980 conference had no such declaration.

The superpowers walked into the 1980 sessions with neither SALT II nor a Comprehensive Test Ban Treaty ratified. The United States, Great Britain, France, and the Soviet Union had not even slowed the pace of their nuclear weapons tests since the 1975 conference.

The United States tried vainly to contain the political damage and extract a final declaration of commitment to nonproliferation, but the nonweapons states, particularly those from the Nonaligned Movement, would not be put off. Their criticism – that the weapons states had welshed on the disarmament portion of the Nonproliferation Treaty – was strident and to the point.

If anyone had forgotten the crucial link between vertical and horizontal proliferation, the 1980 conference brought the point back home. The nonaligned nations are running out of patience. The farther the weapons states stray from the provisions of the 1970 treaty, the farther will the nonweapons states stray. By 1985, the third Review Conference may well be reviewing a treaty that is not worth the paper on which it is printed.

Not only have the nonweapons states had to learn to live with the bomb, they have had to resist the temptation to acquire nuclear weapons. And the superpowers, of all nations, have been the most guilty of chipping away at that resistance.

While preaching to others that the bomb has no political or military value, the superpowers have energetically developed nuclear war fighting capabilities which give the dangerous impression that weapons of mass destruction can achieve political and military objectives. So if the United States and the Soviet Union believe they can employ weapons in a limited, rational manner to coerce one another, why can't India and Pakistan believe the same? If the United States and the Soviet Union believe that nuclear war is survivable and winnable, why can't Brazil and Argentina believe the same?

The superpowers can no longer afford to ignore the link between vertical and horizontal proliferation. The possibility that a regional flareup can result in a nuclear flareup is no longer remote. The Falkland Islands crisis, which no one expected, has demonstrated that the unexpected can happen. That war pitted Great Britain, a nuclear power, against Argentina, an aspiring nuclear power. If Argentina had possessed the bomb during the Falkland Islands war, it may have used it.

Clearly, if the United States and the Soviet Union want to become serious about stopping horizontal proliferation, they will have to stop vertical proliferation. They must halt the nuclear arms race.

Enough is Enough

The nightmare of nuclear war, which has prompted protests by hundreds of thousands of Europeans, has now begun to stir the grass roots in the United States. All across the country religious leaders, business executives, lawyers, doctors, college students, local legislators, and ordinary citizens are organizing to demand a halt to the nuclear arms race. For more than a quarter century Americans have left it up to the experts to grapple with the problem. Now Americans have decided to do something themselves about the threat of nuclear war. Why? Because they are afraid.

Americans want a strong defense, but they are afraid that the $1.7 trillion arms buildup the Reagan Administration plans over five years will only fuel an arms race in which nobody wins. Americans do not want nuclear war, but they hear their leaders talk of ways to wage nuclear war and win. So they have gathered in meeting halls and community centers all over the country to petition the superpowers to stop the arms race.

The Nuclear Freeze Campaign

The initiative gaining the most momentum nationwide is a proposal calling on the United States and the Soviet Union to freeze their nuclear arsenals. The nuclear freeze initiative, says House Speaker O'Neill, is "one of the most remarkable political movements I have ever seen during my years in public service."[4] Freeze groups have been organized in every state, with millions of people signing their petitions. More than 500 town meetings and city councils have endorsed the proposal and almost a dozen state legislatures have either passed or are considering freeze resolutions. The proposals do not ask that the United States unilaterally lay down its arms. No, the proposals come from common-sense people who want *both sides* to stop the arms race.

Congressmen Silvio Conte (Republican-Massachusetts), Jonathan Bingham and I have introduced a similar resolution in the House. It calls on the United States and the Soviet Union to halt the nuclear arms race, to sit down and negotiate a mutual and verifiable freeze on the testing, production, and further deployment of nuclear warheads, missiles, and other delivery systems. The resolution then calls on the superpowers to begin major reductions in their nuclear arsenals. On August 5, 1982, an historic vote was taken in the House on the freeze. Our resolution, which was endorsed by the House Foreign Affairs Committee, lost on the House floor by one vote to a substitute START proposal backed by the Reagan Administration. The vote, however, represented a victory for the freeze. After all, two years ago, at the height of the Reagan arms buildup rhetoric, such a resolution would not have even made it to the House floor for a vote.

In the Senate, twenty-seven senators have also endorsed the freeze resolution, which was introduced by Senators Kennedy and Mark Hatfield (Republican-Oregon). Indeed, it has been Kennedy's strong advocacy of the freeze that has propelled it into the national spotlight. The freeze, under Kennedy's leadership, has become one of the major foreign policy issues of the 1980s.

Because of differences in the superpowers' deployment cycles, there would have to be some give and take at the negotiating table in halting testing, production, and deployment and in cutting back the arsenals. Both sides have concentrated on different weapons systems in building up their nuclear arsenal. The U.S. strategic forces are wisely dispersed on land, submarines, and bombers, while more than three-fourths of the Soviet arsenal is in vulnerable land-based silos. Yet, overall, a "balance of imbalances" now exists between the superpowers.

While the Soviet Union leads the United States in launchers and throw-weight, the United States leads the Soviet Union in warheads (9,000 to 7,000). While the Soviets may lead us in countersilo weapons, we lead them in accurate MIRVed launchers (1,100 to 900). While the Soviet strategic submarine force is large and growing, it is still no match for the U.S. submarine force. Ultimately, both sides have the capacity to reduce the other to rubble. Both sides are and will continue to be vulnerable in certain weapons systems.

Both sides also stand to gain from a freeze and reductions treaty. While the arms buildup has been a drain on the U.S. economy, the Soviets have suffered even more, and a further arms race will cost them dearly. While future developments in first strike weapons will threaten our retaliatory capacity, it will threaten the Soviets' even more because their missiles are primarily land-based. And while Moscow has its hardliners just as Washington does, there is little evidence that the Soviet leadership believes it can win and survive an all-out nuclear war with the United States.

Granted, the process of implementing a freeze and reductions treaty will be arduous and detailed. The agreement will have to be verifiable and that requirement will certainly keep the negotiators busy. But we have no choice but to begin the process, for the arms race is quickly getting out of control. We are approaching the point where technological developments in the weapons systems of both sides have advanced so far and so quickly that it may become extremely difficult in the future to negotiate verifiable treaties. If we deploy, for example, ground- and submarine-launched cruise missiles in large numbers, as the Reagan Administration proposes, we present monumental verification problems for the negotiators, as these relatively small strategic weapons can be easily hidden and therefore would be difficult to count. A freeze, on the other hand, would alleviate much of the verification problem. Because a freeze would stop all activities in weapons programs, the detection of just one cruise missile would be enough to prove a violation.

A nuclear weapons freeze and reductions treaty should not be the only agreement we negotiate with the Soviets. Both sides have been energetically pursuing destabilizing non-nuclear weapons technologies, such as antisubmarine and antisatellite warfare. The superpowers must begin negotiating agreements that put a lid on these dangerous weapons so that the invulnerable deterrence both sides now have with their nuclear submarines and the warning systems both have with their satellites in outer space are preserved.

As it stands, the United States and the Soviet Union are headed for what might be called the "future shock" of the nuclear arms race. Both are poised to deploy large numbers of deadly, provocative weapons that will put a hair trigger on deterrence. Both are approaching the point where they and the rest of the world may be consumed by the nuclear arsenals.

The Reagan Administration entered the White House oblivious to this nuclear collision course. It first proposed to launch a nuclear arms race to force the Soviets to the negotiating table to bargain for deep cuts. (The Reagan deep cuts proposal is acronymed START for Strategic Arms Reduction Talks.) History has shown, however, that stockpiling nuclear bargaining chips against the Soviets does not force them to cut back. The United States, for example, was about five years ahead of the Soviets in MIRV technology in the 1970s. But rather than negotiate a halt to its development, the United States forged ahead with MIRVs hoping that would force the Soviets not to deploy them. The Soviets, however, soon followed suit with their own MIRVs.

As the freeze movement gained strength, the Administration attempted to defuse it by endorsing a "long-term freeze." This would allow the Administration to build more weapons now and freeze later. In other words, it proposed to complete the arms race before going to the negotiating table. The problem is that the arms race can never be completed. When we build more they build more. When we deploy the cruise missile, they will deploy the cruise missile.

The President next proposed in a speech to his alma mater at Eureka College in May 1982 that the United States and the Soviet Union cut their number of strategic ballistic missile warheads by one-third. Each side would be limited to 5,000 warheads with no more than 2,500 of them based on land. The goal of reducing the number of warheads on each side is a worthy one. The Reagan proposal, however, still permits the United States to build destabilizing, first-strike missiles like the MX and the Trident II. The Soviets, in turn, would be allowed to improve their first-strike capacity. The United States also could deploy the cruise missile and the B-1 bomber. In other words, while the Reagan plan cuts back on the number of land- and submarine-based missiles, it still continues the arms race, particularly the qualitative arms race.

Leonid Brezhnev, for his part, has proposed a version of the freeze dealing with the deployment of intermediate-range missiles in Europe and long-range missiles from both sides' strategic arsenals. The Brezhnev proposals have obviously attempted to play to the galleries in Europe and the United States. It now remains to be seen whether the Soviets are serious about stopping the arms race.

The freeze movement can take credit for pushing both sides to the negotiating table. With Reagan offering a reductions proposal and Brezhnev offering a freeze proposal, both sides now have the opportunity to hammer out a treaty that actually halts the arms race and cuts back on the nuclear arsenals. It is now up to the freeze movement to maintain the pressure so both sides remain committed to coming up with a treaty.

Both superpowers must begin to realize that their best defense lies at the negotiating table. The billions of dollars both sides spend on more nuclear weapons does not buy future generations a jot of security. All the world gains is more bombs – most likely in more hands. The nuclear arms race between the superpowers must be stopped, before we blow each other off the face of the earth, and it must be stopped to halt the spread of nuclear weapons among other nations, before they blow themselves off the face of the earth.

PART
4

Conclusion

12

The End
of the Journey

The United States is looking down two paths. The first path is the nuclear path Ronald Reagan would have it follow. The Reagan path continues heavy subsidies for nuclear power at the expense of safer, more efficient energy alternatives. The Reagan path recommits the United States to a vigorous commercial nuclear presence overseas in order to maintain U.S. economic influence among the world's nuclear suppliers. The Reagan path unshackles export restrictions previous administrations placed on nuclear power to contain its dangers. The Reagan path endorses plutonium recycling and, thus, the shortening of the distance between civilian nuclear reactors and nuclear bombs. The Reagan path launches this country on a major nuclear arms buildup that will result in more destabilizing weapons like the MX and Trident II missiles whose purpose is to start nuclear wars, not deter them. At the end of the Reagan path are more nuclear power plants, more nuclear bombs, and more chances of nuclear conflict.

The other path is the non-nuclear path. It is the path toward peace. The world has become entangled in nuclear power and nuclear weapons for all the wrong reasons. It must disentangle from them for all the right reasons.

Nuclear power must be phased out. It must be phased out in the United States, which has three times more reactors than any other country, and it must be phased out in the rest of the world. The United

States cannot continue pouring billions of dollars into domestic nuclear power while hoping that other nations will disavow interest in its bomb-making potential. Whatever economic benefits nuclear power commands, this form of energy is not worth the dangers it poses to world survival. We cannot continue planting bomb factories all over this globe. There is nothing wrong with most commercial products becoming diplomatic tools – so long as the product is wheat, corn, tractors, Ford Granadas, Coca Colas or anything rather than nuclear reactors. Nuclear power is simply too dangerous a commodity to be a bargaining chip in world diplomacy.

Phasing out nuclear power at home and overseas would place major obstacles in the path toward bomb making. Countries would no longer be able to hide bomb making under the cover of a civilian reactor program. The ambiguity would be removed. The goal of any nuclear power initiatives would be clearly military. A country might still attempt to build an explosive device, but the international outlawing of civilian nuclear reactors would up the technical and political ante considerably.[1]

Along with a phaseout of nuclear power, the United States should engage in comprehensive negotiations with the Soviet Union to freeze and reduce the nuclear armaments of both sides. The psychological impetus that the superpowers' arms race gives to horizontal proliferation among other nations can no longer be ignored.

Disentangling ourselves from nuclear power and nuclear bombs will take time. A serious and determined phaseout of nuclear power and a cutback of the nuclear arsenals cannot happen overnight. The process of denuclearization would have to be implemented in an orderly manner. Some actions should be taken today; others should be implemented gradually. I propose a four-point approach:

1. *The United States should establish itself as a nonproliferation leader.* The U.S. government should immediately announce that it intends to phase out nuclear power domestically, to phase out the export of nuclear power overseas, and to urge other countries to join the effort. This should be a clear statement – no hedging with talk of deferrals, no backing down, no concessions that nuclear power might have a future in other parts of the world. While the administration of the phaseout should be flexible, the goal should not be ambiguous. The President should also convene a summit conference with other nuclear supplier nations to begin discussions of a phaseout. Then, as the United States extricates itself from nuclear power, it should begin to wield its diplomatic and economic influence to help other countries phase out nuclear power.

2. *The battle against horizontal proliferation must proceed hand in hand with halting vertical proliferation.* The United States and the Soviet Union must decide when and how to achieve a mutual and verifiable freeze on the testing, production, and further deployment of nuclear warheads, missiles, and other delivery systems. In negotiating a freeze, both countries should give special attention to destabilizing, first-strike weapons or hard-to-verify weapons that would make a freeze difficult to achieve. The two superpowers should then pursue major, mutual, and verifiable reductions in their arsenals. This can be done through annual percentage reductions or equally effective means.

The superpowers should also begin talks on curbing developments in antisatellite and antisubmarine warfare. Proceeding from these bilateral negotiations, multilateral negotiations should begin to halt the further buildup of nuclear arms by the four other weapons states.

3. *The United States should begin the dismantlement of nuclear power at home.* At the outset, the federal government should free nuclear power to meet its maker in the marketplace by halting all subsidies of domestic programs except those essential for public safety, such as regulatory services of the NRC. Subsidies for increased use of light-water reactors, increased uranium enrichment capacity, breeders, and reprocessing facilities should be halted. To help the phaseout, the government should continue to fund programs for disposal of radioactive waste and the decommissioning of worn-out power plants.

The Carter deferral of commercial reprocessing and breeder reactors should be made an outright ban. Barnwell should remain padlocked. Appropriations for Clinch River should be halted. World uranium reserves are more than adequate to fuel present light-water reactors until they become obsolete.

The more than seventy U.S. nuclear power plants should be allowed to continue operating, under close scrutiny and inspection by the NRC, until alternate sources of energy are available. The estimated seventy nuclear plants under construction should be converted to coal plants wherever possible. No new nuclear plant construction permits should be granted. The only exception to this ban on nuclear power might be laboratories conducting scientific or medical research.

4. *The United States should get out of the nuclear export business.* The U.S. government should not renege on its current foreign commitments for nonweapons usable fuel or technology. Subsidies and financial agreements for cooperation should be continued for the life of the reactors or the contract. The United States should also honor previous nuclear supply agreements with other countries. But subsidies should not extend beyond the agreements and should not be made for

exports of *new* equipment, technology, or reactors. Meanwhile, the guillotine provision of the Nonproliferation Act should be strictly enforced. Nuclear commerce should be terminated with countries that do not accept full-scope IAEA safeguards on their facilities. No more exceptions should be made. No more Tarapurs. We also should never again allow ourselves to be blackmailed, as we were with India, by spent fuel overseas. The United States should begin now to retrieve its spent fuel from foreign reactors so countries cannot threaten to reprocess it if the United States does not continue to supply them. The United States also should no longer provide any support for civil reprocessing or breeder reactor development overseas. Eventually, no export licenses should be granted for fuel and equipment to expand a country's nuclear program or to establish a program in a country that does not have one.

Critics will attack these proposals generally for three reasons:

- The United States has developed nuclear power to help achieve "energy independence." In a world starved for more energy, why shouldn't other countries do the same?

- The United States has no means of making the rest of the world pay attention to a phaseout proposal.

- A freeze on nuclear weapons would lock the United States into a position of military disadvantage and vulnerability.

As for the first criticism, the world is in a mad scramble for energy resources. But at home and abroad, nuclear power has played only a small role in meeting energy demand and will likely play a smaller role in the future. As demand for electricity has decreased and costs for reactor construction and operation have increased, nuclear power has witnessed a shrinking market for its product overseas, among both industrialized and developing nations. Indeed, nuclear power's greatest enemy at home and abroad is the free market, in which it is withering away at the hands of other energy sources that are less expensive. Therefore, rather than mourn its loss, pretend it is not happening, or, even worse, attempt to resuscitate it with government subsidies, the world should welcome nuclear power's death by market forces.[2]

A nuclear phaseout, nevertheless, is doomed to failure unless it addresses the desire of nations, ours included, to become energy self-sufficient. If the United States asks other countries to forego nuclear power, it better be ready to offer alternatives. Countries such as Spain, Taiwan, and South Korea will cry "foul," and rightly so, if the United

States, which introduced them to nuclear power and freely supplied them, reverses direction and abandons them.

So far, the United States has made only a token effort to promote other energy sources overseas. As it phases out nuclear power here and abroad, the United States must usher in a worldwide non-nuclear marketing strategy as intense as past huckstering of atomic reactors. In developing countries, the salesmen must begin admitting that atomic reactors do not necessarily bring energy independence. For example, three-fourths of the plant components and materials for a developing country's first reactor will likely have to be imported.

With a phaseout of nuclear energy, there would likely have to be an increased reliance for the short term on coal as a bridge fuel to lead the world into more diversified and efficient energy sources. Coal, with all of its environmental problems, still does not approach the threat that nuclear power and nuclear proliferation pose. Then, under a "soft energy path," as Amory Lovins has described it, nuclear power's contribution to world energy needs could easily be replaced by decentralized and more economical energy sources, such as conservation and the renewables (solar, biomass, hydro, and geothermal power).[3]

The second criticism—that no one in the international community would observe our call for a phaseout—is one the nuclear industry enjoys spreading.

It goes something like this: Because of its ruinous nonproliferation policies, the United States in the past decade has relinquished much of its leadership role in nuclear power to other nations, such as the French and the British, and, worst of all, the Soviets. Consequently, the United States lacks the leverage to impose its will on foreign nuclear programs. If the United States unilaterally phased out its own nuclear power, it would simply deal itself out of any influence it might have and leave control of nuclear weapons to other less nonproliferation-conscious suppliers. Therefore, the only way the United States can hope to retain control over the spread of nuclear terror is to remain a reliable supplier.

The criticism assumes, however, an impotence in U.S. foreign policy that does not exist. The United States is an economic, political, and military giant. Very few steps it takes in any of these three areas do not have consequences in other parts of the world.

To claim that a U.S. declaration of nuclear phaseout would be a unilateral action other countries would disregard overlooks the substantial leadership role our country has in world affairs. When the U.S. government talks, people listen. World energy policy in large part is determined by U.S. energy policy. Even though its export market has shrunk, the United States (which still captured 61 percent of the overseas reactor sales in the past decade) exerts considerable influence over foreign nuclear programs through service and supply pipelines established in previous agreements. Also, it is important to realize that even though they are big-ticket items, atomic reactors are not the only commodities shipped overseas.

The U.S. has fastened its leverage over foreign nuclear programs on a reliable supplier mechanism. By remaining a reliable supplier, the State Department believes it can maintain leverage over nuclear programs and proliferation abroad. The problem, as Tarapur showed, is that the State Department utilizes the supplies but never the leverage.[a]

The United States still has an array of levers other than nuclear power plants, which it can pull to influence international nonproliferation policy. Already on the books is the Symington Amendment to the Foreign Assistance Act, which had previously barred economic and military aid to Pakistan, for example, because it imported uranium enrichment equipment.[b] Congressman Clarence Long, a Maryland Democrat, has suggested another measure to ensure that foreign aid does not indirectly support nuclear power. Long, who is chairman of the Foreign Operations Subcommittee of the House Appropriations Committee, proposed in a 1977 magazine article that foreign aid laws—such as the Foreign Assistance Act, the Export-Import Bank Act, and the Commodity Credit Corporation Charter Act—be amended so a country's aid is reduced in proportion to the amount of money it spends to expand its nuclear power capacity.[4]

The third criticism—that a freeze places the United States in a dangerous military imbalance with the Soviets—has been vigorously pushed by the Reagan Administration. President Reagan claims that the Soviets have gained a "definite margin of superiority."[5] The United States, he maintains, must therefore build up its nuclear forces to catch up with the Soviets before it talks about freezing.

The Soviets, however, have no margin of superiority. While each side leads the other in certain weapons, a rough parity exists between the

[a]India is no novice when it comes to leverage. "About two or three years ago," Congressman Richard Ottinger said during the House's Tarapur debate, "we had a contract with India for . . . the supply of Rhesus monkeys for our research. There was a clause in that contract that said if we used these monkeys for development of weaponry that the contract would be canceled. The Indians discovered that, in fact, we were using some of these monkeys for weaponry development and they immediately cut off our supply of monkeys."

[b]The Reagan Administration, however, was able to get Congress to water down the Symington Amendment so the White House could offer Pakistan $3 billion in military and economic aid to counter the Soviet occupation of Afghanistan.

superpowers. While the Soviets have built up their nuclear forces in the past decade, we have not sat still in modernizing and strengthening ours. While Administration officials talk about U.S. nuclear forces being inferior to the Soviets', no one in the Pentagon would trade the American force for the Soviets'. Indeed, in terms of retaliatory capacity, the United States is in a much better position than the Soviet Union because U.S. warheads are more widely dispersed on land, bombers, and submarines. Even under the worst-case nuclear scenario, in which the Soviets were able to stage a near-perfect first strike, the United States still retains enough nuclear firepower from its submarines to effectively destroy the Soviet Union. Claiming that the Soviets have a margin of superiority does a great disservice to our military posture. The danger is not that we are militarily inferior to the Soviets. The danger is that the Soviets might begin believing misleading statements about U.S. inferiority. So far, they have not.

The Reagan Administration must begin to realize that the problem with the arms race is not who is ahead of whom in a particular weapon. The problem with the arms race is the arms race and that is what the freeze movement wants halted. "What possibly can be wrong with heeding the call, stopping the arms race and proceeding with substantial reductions?" asks Paul C. Warnke, former director of the Arms Control and Disarmament Agency. "I haven't yet heard a good answer. I don't think there is one."[6]

But is a phaseout of nuclear power and a halting of nuclear proliferation politically achievable? Can a Congress and Executive Branch so committed to nuclear power and nuclear weapons development in the past and for the future be turned around? Can the air be cleared of decades of industry inculcation of nuclear power's benefits?

Another disaster like Three Mile Island might be all it takes to kill nuclear power. Or worse, a Pakistan might detonate an atomic device, a Quaddafi might finally buy the bomb, a nuclear terrorist group might hold a city hostage with more than an empty threat. The likelihood increases by the day.

But do we have to wait until a city is evacuated because another reactor spins out of control? Are our political mechanisms so unresponsive that it would take a mad bomber lobbing a nuclear weapon to bring about change? Not if the public demands otherwise. The prescription may be a hackneyed but it is true: Change begins at the grass roots.

But is the public up to battling the nuclear status quo in industry and government? Nuclear power plants are imposing sights. The technology is exceedingly complex, and the average citizen sitting in the audience of a local NRC hearing might cower at the avalanche of scientific jargon. A gut feeling that nuclear power is dangerous can be easily overwhelmed by platoons of engineers with calculators and MIT degrees. The public, however, is not as ignorant about nuclear power and nuclear bombs as the nuclear establishment makes it out to be.

Nuclear power has always pitted the information monopoly of the insiders (industry and government "experts") against the outsiders (the persistent doubters from the grass roots). For a quarter of a century, businesses and governments across the world have accepted the scientific pronouncements of nuclear advocates that the atom is safe and productive. "Convinced of this by their own knowledge and experience," states the Harvard Energy Report, nuclear power's scientific community grew "impatient with outsiders who raised questions." The experts also convinced business and government that opposition to nuclear power was "confined to a comparative handful of noisy and misguided people," the report says. "But the outside doubts would not go away; in fact, they grew in both numbers and intensity as the years passed."[7]

In the same way, the State Department has been afflicted with a smugness that excludes from the proliferation debate anyone who does not carry a diplomatic pouch. "Tarapur is an insider's issue, to which you do not belong, Congressman Markey. If you only knew what State knows, Congressman Markey, you would not oppose shipping thirty-eight tons of uranium to India. You are being simplistic in your opposition, congressman. The experts know best."

No, they do not.

The experts created the terror. The experts spread the terror. The outsiders must now repair the damage.

The grass roots, however, has been divided in its concern over the nuclear peril. In one corner sits the traditional antinuclear movement, which, since Three Mile Island, has built up a large following opposed to domestic nuclear power because of its operational, waste, and economic problems. In another corner sits a reemerging nuclear disarmament movement, the most vocal of which is the nuclear weapons freeze coalition that wants to stop the arms race between the superpowers. And floating in the middle has been the largely ignored issue of horizontal proliferation. While there has been some intermingling, the two movements have gone separate ways. Because many of its members oppose nuclear power but favor a beefed-up defense, the antinuclear movement has largely shunned the disarmament movement. Likewise, the disarmament movement contains many members who oppose nuclear weapons but not civilian nuclear power. Meanwhile, horizontal proliferation has remained a footnote concern to both the disarmers and the antinukers.

What is needed now is a merger of movements. There must be a recognition that any form of nuclear fission, be it controlled in a civilian reactor or uncontrolled in a nuclear explosion, poses unacceptable dangers. The disarmament movement must now realize that at the source of the problem with nuclear bombs is nuclear power. Likewise, the antinuclear movement must now realize that the ultimate problem with nuclear power is nuclear bombs, be they stockpiled by the weapons states or proliferated among the nonweapons states.

Washington's public interest and environmental lobbies in particular must reassess their priorities and direct their efforts on Capitol Hill toward the proliferation dangers of nuclear power. Radioactive waste, reactor safety, and poor economics are all valid concerns the antinuclear lobby should impress upon Congressmen. But the real danger with nuclear power plants is that they can be converted into bomb factories, and the lobby must now drive this point home.

The crusade to phase out nuclear power and the proliferation dangers it poses will need the perseverance of the CSE volunteers who dogged candidates from one campaign stop to another. It will need more peaceful marches, more letterwriting, and more organizing. It will need more rallies like the one in New York where almost a million people gathered for one of the largest demonstrations in U.S. history and called for a freeze on the arms race. It may even need unorthodox stunts like radioactive peanuts and students dressed in gorilla suits or an underage congressman running for vice president.

Above all, the campaign needs you. If nuclear power and nuclear weapons proliferation concern you, or if they scare you, do not allow the experts to brush you off. Trust your instincts. Raise your hand at a public hearing and don't sit down until you are satisfied with the answer. Sign a freeze petition. Write your congressman, or better yet, round up a friend or two who believes as you do and meet your congressman face to face. Representatives and senators are busy people, so be stubborn. Keep in mind that most politicians, as I have found, actually do not believe strongly one way or the other on the issue of nuclear power. On most House votes, the majority will side with industry, not out of any conviction, but by default because no one, especially constituents, has flooded them with the opposing arguments.

Nuclear proliferation is a problem too long ignored. Now, before it is too late, the public must draw the line. The stakes are high. In 1946, Bernard Baruch warned the United Nations: "We are here to make a choice between the quick and the dead. That is our business."[8]

That is still our business today.

APPENDIXES

Appendix A

UNITED STATES OF AMERICA
NUCLEAR REGULATORY COMMISSION

COMMISSIONERS:

John F. Ahearne, Chairman
Victor Gilinsky
Richard T. Kennedy
Joseph M. Hendrie
Peter A. Bradford

In the Matter of	License Nos.XSNM-1379
	XSNM-1569
EDLOW INTERNATIONAL COMPANY	XCOM-0240
	XCOM-0250
(Agent for the Government of India	XCOM-0376
on Applications to Export Special	XCOM-0381
Nuclear Materials and Components)	XCOM-0395

MEMORANDUM AND ORDER
CLI-80-18

Edlow International Company, as agent for the Government of India, filed the following license applications with the Commission seeking authorization to export materials and components for use in the Tarapur Atomic Power Station (Tarapur) located near Bombay, India:

(1) XSNM-1379 on November 1, 1977 for export of 487.3 kilograms of U-235 contained in 19,858.8 kilograms of uranium enriched to a maximum of 2.7%;

(2) XCOM-0240 on April 25, 1979, as amended May 8, 1980, for export of replacement parts;

(3) XCOM-0250 on May 7, 1979 for export of replacement parts;

(4) XSNM-1569 on August 17, 1979 for export of 487.3 kilograms of U-235 contained in 19,858.8 kilograms of uranium enriched to a maximum of 2.7%;

(5) XCOM-0376 on March 6, 1980 for export of replacement parts;

(6) XCOM-0381 on March 14, 1980 for export of replacement parts; and

(7) XCOM-0395 on April 3, 1980 for export of replacement parts.

The lengthy history of U.S.-Indian cooperation in connection with the Tarapur reactors is fully chronicled in several formal Commission decisions.[1]

The Commission cannot find, based on a reasonable judgment of the assurances provided by the Government of India and other information available, that License Applications XSNM-1379, XSNM-1569, XCOM-0240, XCOM-0250, XCOM-0376, XCOM-0381 and XCOM-0395 meet the criteria for issuance set forth in Sections 109, 127, and 128 of the Atomic Energy Act. Accordingly, NRC is referring these license applications to the President, pursuant to procedures set forth in Section 126b.(2) of the Atomic Energy Act.

The basis for the Commission's decision is as follows. India has several nuclear facilities which have not been placed under International Atomic Energy Agency safeguards. After reviewing the legislative history of Section 128 of the Atomic Energy Act, the Commission has concluded that the full-scope safeguards criterion applies to the two fuel applications. The legislative history of the Nuclear Non-Proliferation Act is replete with references that the full-scope safeguards criterion would come into effect at a date certain[2]– that the application of the criterion would have a "guillotine" effect.[3] The State Department's view that the criterion does not apply to license applications filed before September 10, 1979 where the applicant reasonably expected the license to issue prior to March 10, 1980 is, we

[1]CLI-76-10, 4 NRC 1 (1976); CLI-76-6, 3 NRC 563 (1976); CLI-77-20, 5 NRC 1358 (1977); CLI-78-8, 7 NRC 436 (1978); CLI-78-20, 8 NRC 675 (1978); CLI-79-4, 9 NRC 209 (1979).

[2]*E.g.,* H. Rep. No. 95-587, 95th Cong., 1st Sess. at 22, S. Rep. No. 95-467, 95th Cong. 1, 1st Sess. at 18; Statement of Senator Glenn, 123 Cong. Rec. S. 13139 (July 29, 1977).

[3]Testimony of Joseph Nye, Deputy Undersecretary of State for Security Assistance, Science and Technology, before the Subcommittees on International Security and Scientific Affairs, and on International Economic Policy and Trade of the House Committee on International Relations, 95th Cong., 1st Sess., at 118 (May 19, 1977).

believe, inconsistent with Congressional intent. As we understand the Department's view, if an application were filed with the Commission prior to September 10, 1979, an applicant expected the license before March 10, 1980, but the Executive Branch did not provide the Commission with its views until years later, the criterion would not apply. Such results do not comport with the "guillotine" approach which was contemplated.

Because of unique features in the Agreement for Cooperation between the United States and India, the Commission is also unable to find that the two fuel applications satisfy the requirements of Section 127 of the Atomic Energy Act or that the component applications satisfy the requirements of Section 109 of the Atomic Energy Act. This issue is thoroughly discussed in earlier Commission opinions.[4]

The Commission's inability to issue these licenses should not be read as a recommendation one way or the other on the proposed exports. Rather, we have found that the particular statutory findings with which the NRC is charged cannot be made. Congress provided that the President may in such a case authorize the export by executive order if he finds "that withholding the proposed export would be seriously prejudicial to the achievement of United States nonproliferation objectives, or would otherwise jeopardize the common defense and security."*

It is so ORDERED.

By the Commission
SAMUEL J. CHALK
Secretary of the Commission

Dated at Washington, D.C.
this 16th day of May, 1980.

Author's note: In addition to the two licenses for thirty-eight tons of enriched uranium, the NRC disapproved five other licenses for spare parts for the Tarapur plant. The House and Senate, however, decided early on to allow the shipment of the spare parts as a goodwill gesture.

[4]CLI-78-8, 7 NRC 436 (1977); CLI-79-4, 9 NRC 209 (1979).

*Section 201 of the Energy Reorganization Act, 42 U.S.C. 5841, provides that action of the Commission shall be determined by a "majority vote of the members present." Commissioner Kennedy was not present at the meeting at which this Order was approved. Had he been present he would have voted to approve this Order. Accordingly, the formal vote of the Commission is 4-0.

Appendix B

The Nuclear Fuel Cycle

For the laymen who, like I, struggled through high school physics and quickly proceeded to forget most of what they did manage to learn, here is a quick refresher course on your friend, the atom.

An atom is made up of three subatomic particles—protons and neutrons, clumped together in the nucleus of the atom, and electrons that spin around the nucleus. The nucleus is held together by what physicists call the "strong" force. If the nucleus of the atom is split, energy is released.

Most natural substances are made up of stable atoms whose nuclei are extremely difficult to split. However, several elements, such as uranium, are very heavy (their nuclei are made up of a lot of protons and neutrons), and compared to lighter atoms, are not held together very tightly. These elements can be split when hit by a neutron.

The United States has the largest uranium reserves in the world, at least 300,000 tons that can be easily extracted and up to two million tons that is recoverable if the price is right. About one-half comes from underground mines; the rest is strip mined.

This natural uranium ore is made up of two types of uranium, called isotopes. One isotope is Uranium-238 (U-238), which has 92 protons and 146 neutrons (for a total of 238 subatomic particles in its nucleus). The other isotope is Uranium-235 (U-235), which has 92 protons and 143 neutrons. The two isotopes differ in the ease with which their nuclei can be split by a neutron. Uranium-235 can be easily split (it is fissile, according to scientific jargon), while U-238 is not easily split (it is fertile).

Uranium ore from the mines contains less than 1 percent U-235, the fissile isotope that is easy to split, and more than 99 percent U-238, the fertile isotope that is difficult to split. In order to be used for most reactors, the uranium must have a concentration of about 3 percent U-235. A crude nuclear bomb requires a concentration of at least 10 percent or more. The high-grade nuclear weapons contain more than 90 percent concentration of U-235.

To increase its concentration of U-235, uranium must be enriched.[a] There are four ways this can be done—by gaseous diffusion, the most

---

[a]For simplicity's sake, I have left out certain steps of what scientists call "nuclear fuel cycle," the process of converting uranium to reactor-grade fuel, running it through the reactor, and disposing of the spent fuel.

popular of the four; by gas centrifuge enrichment, which is beginning to be used in Europe; by various aerodynamic methods, which have been tested in West Germany and South Africa; and by laser techniques, still under research.

Sounds complicated? It is. Each procedure requires a lot of money, a lot of equipment, and a lot of technical know-how.

The important thing for the layman to remember is that each method is capable of enriching uranium not only for nuclear reactors, but also for nuclear bombs.

Once the uranium is enriched, it is processed into reactor fuel. About three-fourths of the reactors worldwide are light-water reactors, which have been developed in the United States.[b] A light-water reactor uses water heated to steam by the nuclear chain reaction. The steam then turns a turbine generator to produce electricity.

Here is what happens in a chain reaction:

- A neutron hits a U-235 isotope, splitting it into two lighter elements – for example a barium atom and a krypton atom. The splitting of the U-235 creates energy, a tremendous amount of energy. One-tenth of an ounce of U-235 generates enough electricity to keep 10,000 light bulbs glowing for a day.

- When U-235 splits, it also gives off two or three neutrons, which, in turn, split another U-235. This is the chain reaction, which, in a reactor, is controlled and, in nuclear explosives, is not.

- Not all the spare neutrons strike U-235. Some hit the fertile U-238, which, when it absorbs the neutron, becomes plutonium-239.

The plutonium-239, which is fissile, can then be separated from the spent fuel through a mechanical and chemical technique known as reprocessing. It can then be reused as reactor fuel. It can also be used, however, to fabricate nuclear bombs.

[b]Not all reactors use enriched uranium. Heavy-water reactors, developed and marketed primarily by the Canadians, consume natural uranium with deuterium (heavy water) used as a moderator and coolant. India's nuclear explosion in 1974 diverted plutonium from a heavy-water research reactor Canada had supplied.

Appendix C

EXECUTIVE ORDER
EXPORT OF SPECIAL NUCLEAR MATERIAL AND COMPONENTS TO INDIA

By the authority vested in me as President by the Constitution and statutes of the United States of America, including Section 126b(2) of the Atomic Energy Act of 1954, as amended (42 U.S.C. 2155(b)(2)), and having determined that withholding the exports proposed pursuant to Nuclear Regulatory Commission export license applications XSNM-1379, XSNM-1569, XCOM-0240, XCOM-0250, XCOM-0376, XCOM-0381, and XCOM-0395, would be seriously prejudicial to the achievement of United States nonproliferation objectives and would otherwise jeopardize the common defense and security, those exports to India are authorized; however, such exports shall not occur for a period of 60 days as defined by Section 130g of the Atomic Energy Act of 1954, as amended (42 U.S.C. 2159(g)).

JIMMY CARTER

THE WHITE HOUSE, June 19, 1980.

JUNE 19, 1980, MESSAGE FROM THE PRESIDENT, AUTHORIZING THE EXPORT OF SPECIAL NUCLEAR MATERIAL AND COMPONENTS TO INDIA

To the Congress of the United States:

I am transmitting with this message, pursuant to Section 126b(2) of the Atomic Energy Act of 1954, as amended, an Executive Order authorizing the export of 39,718 kgs. of low-enriched uranium to India for use in fueling its Tarapur Atomic Power Station and authorizing the export of replacement parts for this station.

Two applications for licenses to export the fuel were submitted to the Nuclear Regulatory Commission in September 1978 and August 1979 respectively. After a careful review of these applications, and the applications for replacement parts of the Tarapur reactors, the Executive Branch concluded that the proposed exports would not be inimical to the common defense and security, that they met all applicable statutory criteria under the Atomic Energy Act, and that the licenses should be issued. The Commission was notified of these Executive Branch findings and recommendations on March 28, 1979, and on May 7, 1980.

On May 16, 1980, the Nuclear Regulatory Commission decided that it could not find that the criteria for issuing the licenses had been met. Pursuant to the law, the Commission then referred these applications to me.

In reaching its decision, the Commission argued that the full-scope safeguards export criterion of Section 128a of the Atomic Energy Act applies to these applications because they do not fall within the grace period provided in the law. The Department of State, on the other hand, concludes that this statutory criterion does not apply to these two applications because they were submitted before September 10, 1979, the cut-off date specified in the law, because the first shipment under each was reasonably planned to occur before March 10, 1980, and because there is no reason to believe that the applications were filed early as a way of circumventing the September 10, 1979, deadline.

In any event, the license criteria specified by statute, of which Section 128a is one, are not the same as the export criteria on the basis of which I must determine whether to issue an Executive Order. As the Commission noted, its inability to issue the licenses "should not be read as a recommendation one way or the other on the proposed exports." As the Commission noted further, in such cases the law provides that the President may authorize such exports by Executive Order if he determines that withholding them would be seriously prejudicial to the achievement of United States nonproliferation objectives or would otherwise jeopardize the common defense and security.

I have determined that to withhold these exports would be seriously prejudicial to the achievement of United States nonproliferation objectives and would otherwise jeopardize the common defense and security. I have made this determination for the policy reasons discussed below. However, I want to make it clear that I do in fact regard these export applications as having fallen within the statutory grace period before the full-scope safeguards requirement of action 128a takes effect. Thus, my authorization of these exports does not constitute a precedent for an exception to the full-scope safeguards criterion. Further, this action in no way indicates a change in the high priority I attach to preventing the spread of nuclear explosives. On the contrary, this action reflects my judgment that nonproliferation would be set back, not advanced, by withholding these exports, and that our failure to supply this fuel could seriously jeopardize other important U.S. interests.

India's failure to accept international safeguards on all its peaceful nuclear activities and its failure to commit itself not to conduct further nuclear explosions are of serious concern to me. These exports will help us to maintain a dialogue with India in which we try to narrow our differences on these issues.

The exports will avoid the risk of a claim by India that the United States has broken an existing agreement between the two governments and has thereby relieved India of its obligation to refrain from reprocessing the fuel previously supplied by the United States.

Supply of this fuel will also ensure the continuation of safeguards and other U.S. controls on disposition of U.S. origin fuel that has been supplied to India.

Approval of these exports will help strengthen ties with a key South Asian democracy at a time when it is particularly important for us to do so. Insecurity in South and Southwest Asia has been greatly heightened by the crisis in Iran and the Soviet invasion of Afghanistan. We must do all we reasonably can to promote stability in the area and to bolster our relations with states there, particularly those that can play a role in checking Soviet expansion.

When I signed the Nuclear Nonproliferation Act of 1978, I expressed reservations about the constitutionality of provisions of law which purport to allow the Congress to overturn my decisions by actions not subject to my veto power. In transmitting this Executive Order, I also want to make it clear that I am not departing from those reservations.

JIMMY CARTER

THE WHITE HOUSE, June 19, 1980.

Appendix D

96TH CONGRESS
2D SESSION

H. CON. RES. 367

Disapproving the proposed export to India of low-enriched uranium for the Tarapur Atomic Power Station pursuant to export license application XSNM–1569.

IN THE HOUSE OF REPRESENTATIVES

JUNE 19, 1980

Mr. BINGHAM (for himself, Mr. ZABLOCKI, Mr. WOLFF, Mr. FASCELL, Mr. BROOMFIELD, Mr. DERWINSKI, Mr. WOLPE, Mr. ROSENTHAL, Mr. FINDLEY, Mr. LAGOMARSINO, Mr. STUDDS, Mr. BARNES, and Mr. WINN) submitted the following concurrent resolution; which was referred to the Committee on Foreign Affairs

---

CONCURRENT RESOLUTION

Disapproving the proposed export to India of low-enriched uranium for the Tarapur Atomic Power Station pursuant to export license application XSNM–1569.

1   *Resolved by the House of Representatives (the Senate*

2   *concurring),* That the Congress does not favor the proposed

3   export of low-enriched uranium to India pursuant to export

4   license application XSNM–1569 which would be authorized

5   by the Executive order transmitted to the Congress by the

6   President on June 19, 1980.

Author's note: Bingham introduced two disapproval resolutions, one for each of the two export license applications of nineteen tons of enriched uranium.

96TH CONGRESS
2D SESSION

H. CON. RES. 368

Disapproving the proposed export to India of low-enriched uranium for the
Tarapur Atomic Power Station pursuant to export license application
XSNM–1379.

IN THE HOUSE OF REPRESENTATIVES

JUNE 19, 1980

Mr. BINGHAM (for himself, Mr. ZABLOCKI, Mr. WOLFF, Mr. FASCELL, Mr.
BROOMFIELD, Mr. DERWINSKI, Mr. WOLPE, Mr. ROSENTHAL, Mr. FIND-
LEY, Mr. LAGOMARSINO, Mr. STUDDS, Mr. BARNES, and Mr. WINN) submitted the following concurrent resolution; which was referred to the Committee
on Foreign Affairs

CONCURRENT RESOLUTION

Disapproving the proposed export to India of low-enriched uranium for the Tarapur Atomic Power Station pursuant to
export license application XSNM–1379.

1   *Resolved by the House of Representatives (the Senate*

2   *concurring)*, That the Congress does not favor the proposed

3   export of low-enriched uranium to India pursuant to export

4   license application XSNM–1379 which would be authorized

5   by the Executive order transmitted to the Congress by the

6   President on June 19, 1980.

96TH CONGRESS
2D SESSION

H. CON. RES. 372

Disapproving the proposed exports to India of low-enriched uranium for the Tarapur Atomic Power Station.

IN THE HOUSE OF REPRESENTATIVES

JUNE 23, 1980

Mr. MARKEY (for himself, Mr. WAXMAN, Mr. KEMP, Mr. EDWARDS of Oklahoma, Mr. WOLPE, Mr. SHANNON, Mrs. CHISHOLM, Mr. BONIOR of Michigan, Mr. FAZIO, Mr. BEDELL, Mr. MITCHELL of Maryland, Mr. STARK, Mr. OTTINGER, Mr. MOTTL, Mr. LEACH of Iowa, Mr. MAGUIRE, Mr. HINSON, Mr. OBERSTAR, Mr. NOLAN, Mr. ERDAHL, Mr. SOLOMON, Mr. WEISS, Mr. McKINNEY, Mr. GREEN, Mr. PORTER, Mr. ADDABBO, Mr. DRINAN, Mr. RATCHFORD, Mr. ROYER, Mr. GRAY, Mr. BROWN of California, Mr. EDGAR, Mr. KOSTMAYER, and Mr. VENTO) submitted the following concurrent resolution; which was referred to the Committee on Foreign Affairs

---

CONCURRENT RESOLUTION

Disapproving the proposed exports to India of low-enriched uranium for the Tarapur Atomic Power Station.

1 *Resolved by the House of Representatives (the Senate*
2 *concurring)*, That the Congress does not favor the proposed
3 exports of low-enriched uranium to India which would be
4 authorized by the Executive order transmitted to the Con-
5 gress by the President on June 19, 1980.

96TH CONGRESS
2D SESSION

S. CON. RES. 109

[Report No. 96–939]

Disapproving the proposed export to India of low-enriched uranium for the Tarapur Atomic Power Station pursuant to export license applications XSNM–1379 and XSNM–1569.

IN THE SENATE OF THE UNITED STATES

JULY 25 (legislative day, JUNE 12), 1980

Mr. GLENN (for himself, Mr. RIBICOFF, Mr. CRANSTON, Mr. HARRY F. BYRD, JR., Mr. BOSCHWITZ, Mr. COHEN, Mr. CANNON, Mr. DOLE, Mr. GOLDWATER, Mr. HEFLIN, Mr. LEAHY, Mr. METZENBAUM, Mr. PROXMIRE, Mr. LAXALT, Mr. HATFIELD, and Mr. THURMOND) submitted the following concurrent resolution; which was referred to the Committee on Foreign Relations

SEPTEMBER 15 (legislative day, JUNE 12), 1980

Reported by Mr. CHURCH, without amendment

SEPTEMBER 24 (legislative day, JUNE 12), 1980

Indefinitely postponed

CONCURRENT RESOLUTION

Disapproving the proposed export to India of low-enriched uranium for the Tarapur Atomic Power Station pursuant to export license applications XSNM–1379 and XSNM–1569.

1   *Resolved by the Senate (the House of Representatives*

2   *concurring)*, That the Congress does not favor the proposed

3   export of low-enriched uranium to India pursuant to export

4   license applications XSNM–1379 and XSNM–1569 which

5   would be authorized by the Executive order transmitted to

6   the Congress by the President on June 19, 1980.

NOTES

CHAPTER ONE

1   Thomas O'Toole, *NRC against U.S. Uranium flow to India,* Washington Post/Los Angeles Times News Service, THE BOSTON GLOBE, 17 May 1980, p. 3.

2   Joanne Omang, *Panel Votes 6-Month Ban on New A-Plants,* THE WASHINGTON POST, 10 May 1979, p. A13.

3   Nuclear Regulatory Commission, Transcript of Proceedings, Washington, D.C., 16 July 1979, p. 48

4   *Angry Kemeny Commission Promises To Recommend Major Changes At NRC,* INSIDE N.R.C. (August 24, 1979): 1.

5   CONGRESSIONAL RECORD, 29 November 1979, p. 11340-61.

6   David Burnham, *Freeze On Building of Nuclear Plants Rejected By House,* THE NEW YORK TIMES, 30 November 1979, p. 1

7   Jonathan Schell, *Reflections: The Fate of the Earth, Part I,* THE NEW YORKER (February 1, 1982): 47.

CHAPTER TWO

1   CONGRESSIONAL RECORD, 17 March 1981, p. 2237.

2   Congressional Research Service, NUCLEAR PROLIFERATION FACTBOOK (Washington, D.C.: Government Printing Office, 1980): 325.

3   David M. Rosenbaum, *Nuclear Terror,* INTERNATIONAL SECURITY 1 (Winter 1977): 140-41.

4   Congressional Research Service, READER ON NUCLEAR PROLIFERATION (Washington, D.C.: Government Printing Office, 1980): 16.

5   Albert Wohlstetter, et al., SWORDS FROM PLOUGHSHARES: THE MILITARY POTENTIAL OF CIVILIAN NUCLEAR ENERGY (Chicago: University of Chicago Press, 1977).

6   Spurgeon M. Keeny, Jr., et al., NUCLEAR POWER ISSUES AND CHOICES, REPORT OF THE NUCLEAR ENERGY AND POLICY STUDY GROUP (Cambridge, Mass.: Ballinger Publishing Company, 1977), p. 332.

7   The Guardian, WINDSCALE: A SUMMARY OF THE EVIDENCE AND THE ARGUMENTS (London: The Guardian Newspapers Limited, 1977) p. 56-57.

8   Congressional Research Service, NUCLEAR WEAPONS PROLIFERATION: LEGISLATION FOR POLICY AND OTHER MEASURES, Issue Brief No. IB77011, (Washington, D.C.: Government Printing Office, November 14, 1978). p. 4.

9   Jimmy Carter, NUCLEAR POWER POLICY, APRIL 7, 1977, Presidential Documents, April 18, 1977, vol. 13, no. 15.

10   Amory B. Lovins, et al., *Nuclear Power and Nuclear Bombs,* FOREIGN AFFAIRS 58 (Summer 1980): 1137.

11   Ibid., p. 1140.

12   Ibid., p. 1142.

13   Ibid.

14   Ibid., p. 1142-43.

15   Ibid., p. 1143.

16   Ibid., p. 1142.

17   Steve Weissman and Herbert Krosney, THE ISLAMIC BOMB (New York: Times Books, 1981), p. 73.

18 World Bank, ENERGY IN THE DEVELOPING COUNTRIES (Washington, D.C.: World Bank, 1980), p. 46.
19 *1980: Bittersweet Times For Uranium*, THE ENERGY DAILY, 18 March 1981, p. 2.
20 World Bank, p. 45.
21 Interview with officials from the Energy Information Administration, April 5, 1982.
22 Washington Analysis Corporation, A subsidiary of Bache, Halsey, Stuart, Shields Incorporated, *Nuclear Energy: Dark Outlook* (Washington, D.C., December 21, 1979): 6-7 (mimeo).
23 Robert Stobaugh and Daniel Yergin, eds., ENERGY FUTURE, Report of the Energy Project at the Harvard Business School (New York: Random House, 1979), p. 264.
24 World Bank, p. 64.
25 Carl Walske, *Nuclear Electric Power and the Proliferation of Nuclear Weapons States*, INTERNATIONAL SECURITY 1, no. 3 (Winter 1977): 106.

CHAPTER THREE

1 Roberta Wohlstetter, *U.S. Peaceful Aid and the Indian Bomb*, in Albert Wohlstetter, et al., NUCLEAR POLICIES: FUEL WITHOUT THE BOMB (Cambridge, Mass.: Ballinger Publishing Company, 1979), ch. 3, pp. 58-59.

CHAPTER FOUR

1 *Nuclear Nearsightedness*, THE WASHINGTON POST, 9 May 1980, p. A22.
2 *This Nuclear Decision Is Contagious*, THE NEW YORK TIMES, 12 May 1980, p. A18.
3 *Nuclear Cave*, THE WALL STREET JOURNAL, 9 May 1980, p. 18.

4 Edward J. Markey, letter to the President, May 22, 1980.
5 Edward J. Markey, *Dear Colleague* to other members of Congress, May 22, 1980.
6 Richard Burt, *U.S. Reported Reviewing Sale of Nuclear Fuel To India*, THE NEW YORK TIMES, 4 June 1980, p. A3.
7 Edward J. Markey, *A Tougher Stand—Starting with India*, THE WASHINGTON POST, 9 June 1980, p. A21.
8 Robert F. Goheen, *Nuclear Fuel to India: Buying Time*, THE WASHINGTON POST, 27 June 1980, p. A10.
9 McGeorge Bundy, *Ship Fuel to India*, THE WASHINGTON POST, 13 June 1980, p. A19.

CHAPTER FIVE

1 U.S. Congress, Senate, Committee on Foreign Relations and Committee on Governmental Affairs, JOINT HEARINGS ON THE ISSUE OF WHETHER TO SHIP NUCLEAR FUEL TO INDIA FOR THE TARAPUR POWER REACTORS, 96th Congress, 2nd Session (Washington, D.C.: Government Printing Office, 1980), p. 65-117.
2 *CBS Evening News*, Transcript of CBS Evening News (New York: CBS, Inc., 19 June 1980).
3 U.S. Congress, House, Committee on Foreign Affairs, HEARINGS AND MARKUP ON H. CON. RES. 367 AND 368, RESOLUTIONS OF DISAPPROVAL PERTAINING TO THE SHIPMENT OF NUCLEAR FUEL TO INDIA, 96th Congress, 2nd Session (Washington, D.C.: Government Printing Office, 1980), p. 1-146.

CHAPTER SIX

1 *1980 Republican Platform Text*, CONGRESSIONAL QUARTERLY WEEKLY REPORT 38, no. 29 (19 July 1980): 2052.

2   Campaign For Safe Energy, *Missing Links in the Chain Reaction: A Summary of the Presidential Candidates' Positions on Nuclear Power* (Boston, 30 May 1980): 12 (Mimeo.).

3   John Herbers, *Nuclear Energy Emerging as a Key Issue in Campaigning for Presidency*, THE NEW YORK TIMES, 21 February 1980, p. B10.

4   Democratic National Committee, OFFICIAL REPORT OF THE PROCEEDINGS OF THE DEMOCRATIC NATIONAL COMMITTEE (Washington, D.C.: Democratic National Committee, 1980), p. 494–96.

CHAPTER SEVEN

1   U.S. Congress, House, Committee on Foreign Affairs, HEARINGS AND MARKUP ON H. CON. RES. 367 AND 368, RESOLUTIONS OF DISAPPROVAL PERTAINING TO THE SHIPMENT OF NUCLEAR FUEL TO INDIA, 96th Congress, 2nd Session (Washington, D.C.: Government Printing Office, 1980), p. 148.

2   *Don't Reload Tarapur*, THE NEW YORK TIMES, 9 September 1980, p. 18.

3   U.S. Congress, Senate, Committee on Foreign Relations, TARAPUR NUCLEAR FUEL EXPORT, REPORT OF THE COMMITTEE ON FOREIGN RELATIONS UNITED STATES SENATE TOGETHER WITH MINORITY VIEWS, 96th Congress, 2nd Session (Washington, D.C.: Government Printing Office, 1980), p. 36–37.

4   Ibid., p. 37–38.

5   U.S. Congress, Senate, Committee on Foreign Relations, OFFICIAL TRANSCRIPT: PROPOSED NUCLEAR FUEL SHIPMENT TO INDIA (TARAPUR) AND THE VOTE ON DISAPPROVING THE SHIPMENT (Washington, D.C., Anderson Reporting, 10 September 1980), 1–36.

6   *India Reacts Calmly to Setback in U.S. on Atom Fuel*, THE NEW YORK TIMES, 12 September 1980, p. A10.

7   Irvin Molotsky *'Nuke Twins' in Congress Lobby for Nuclear Power*, THE NEW YORK TIMES, 7 January 1980, p. D10.

8   Mike McCormack, *Dear Colleague* to other members of Congress, July 14, 1980.

9   *Unreliable Customer*, THE WASHINGTON POST, 12 September 1980, p. A18.

10 John H. Glenn, Jr., *No Fuel for Tarapur*, THE WASHINGTON POST, 22 September 1980, p. A15.

11 *Clear Signals on Nuclear Fuel*, THE WASHINGTON POST, 22 September 1980, p. A15.

12 *Nuclear Hypocrisy*, THE WALL STREET JOURNAL, 24 September 1980, p. 30.

13 Leonard Dowie, Jr., *Swiss Send Nuclear Aid to Pakistan*, THE WASHINGTON POST, 21 September 1980, pp. A1, A21.

14 *Sell Nuclear Fuel to India?* U.S. NEWS & WORLD REPORT (August 18, 1980): 47–48.

15 *Fuel To India*, Transcript of the MacNeil/Lehrer Report (New York: Educational Broadcasting Corporation, September 16, 1980): 1–8.

16 John W. Wydler, *Dear Colleague* to other members of Congress, November 14, 1979.

17 Edward J. Markey, *Dear Colleague* to other members of Congress, September 18, 1980.

18 Judith Miller, *Senate Opens Debate on Uranium Sales to India; Vote Seen as Policy Test*, THE NEW YORK TIMES, 24 September 1980, p. 6

19 THE NEW YORK TIMES, 5 October 1980, Sec. 11, p. 3.

20 CONGRESSIONAL RECORD, 23 September 1980, p. 13211.

CHAPTER EIGHT

1   NUCLEONICS WEEK 21, no. 51 (December 18, 1980): 1.

2   U.S. Congress, Senate, Committee on Foreign Relations and Committee on Governmental Affairs, JOINT HEARINGS ON THE ISSUE OF WHETHER TO SHIP NUCLEAR FUEL TO INDIA FOR THE TARAPUR POWER REACTORS, 96th Congress, 2nd Session (Washington, D.C.: Government Printing Office, 1980), p. 69.

3   Stuart Auerbach, *India Proposing Amicable End to Nuclear Contract,* THE WASHINGTON POST, 4 February 1981, p. A1, A14.

4   Don Oberdorfer, *U.S. Is Ending 18-Year Nuclear Pact With India,* THE WASHINGTON POST, 23 April 1981, p. A19.

5   Congressional Research Service, NUCLEAR EXPORTS: TERMINATION OF U.S. NUCLEAR COOPERATION WITH INDIA, Issue Brief No. IB81087 (Washington, D.C.: Government Printing Office, February 4, 1982): 4.

6   Ibid., p. 5.

7   Victor Gilinsky, Speech before the League of Women Voters Education Fund, Silver Spring, Maryland, November 17, 1980.

8   Congressional Research Service, READER ON NUCLEAR PROLIFERATION (Washington, D.C.: Government Printing Office, 1980): 16.

9   U.S. Congress, Joint Committee on Atomic Energy, ATOMIC POWER AND PRIVATE ENTERPRISE, 82nd Congress, 2nd Session (Washington, D.C.: Government Printing Office, 1952), p. 107.

10 Robert Stobaugh and Daniel Yergin, eds., ENERGY FUTURE, Report of the Energy Project at the Harvard Business School (New York: Random House, 1979), p. 140.

11 Daniel Yergin, *The Terrifying Prospect,* ATLANTIC (April 1977): 53.

12 U.S. Congress, Joint Committee on Atomic Energy, p. 377.

13 U.S. Congress, Joint Committee on Atomic Energy, pp. 24–25.

CHAPTER NINE

1   Saddam Hussein, Statement during Cabinet Meeting June 23, 1981 (Foreign Broadcast Service-MEA-81-121, June 24, 1981).

2   Congressional Research Service, ISRAELI RAID INTO IRAQ, Issue Brief No. IB81103 (Washington, D.C.: Government Printing Office, October 1, 1981): 9.

3   IAEA SAFEGUARDS: AN INTRODUCTION (Vienna, International Atomic Energy Agency, 1981), p. 14.

4   Gary Hart, Testimony before the Subcommittee on International Economic Policy and Trade, Committee on Foreign Affairs, U.S. House of Representatives, Washington, D.C., March 3, 1982.

5   General Accounting Office, Comptroller General, REPORT TO THE CONGRESS: ASSESSMENT OF U.S. AND INTERNATIONAL CONTROLS OVER THE PEACEFUL USES OF NUCLEAR ENERGY (Washington, D.C.: Government Printing Office, September 14, 1976), p. 38.

6   Nunzio Paladino, Chairman, Nuclear Regulatory Commission, letter to Senator Alan Simpson, Chairman Subcommittee on Nuclear Regulation, Committee on Environment and Public Works, U.S. Senate, November 27, 1981.

7   LDC NUCLEAR POWER PROSPECTS, 1975–1990: COMMERCIAL, ECONOMIC AND SECURITY IMPLICATIONS (Washington, D.C.: Energy Research and Development Administration, 1976), p. V-54.

8   Roger Richter, Testimony before the Committee on Foreign Relations, U.S. Senate, Washington, D.C., June 19, 1981.

CHAPTER TEN

1   Robert Lindsay, *Reagan Says America Should Not Bar Others From A-Bomb Output,* THE NEW YORK TIMES, 1 February 1980, p. A12.
2   Ronald Reagan, Statement by the President, Press Release, Office of the Press Secretary, The White House, July 16, 1981, p. 2.
3   Ibid., p. 1.
4   Steven J. Baker, *Arms Transfers ana Nuclear Proliferation,* in William H. Kincade and Jeffrey D. Poro, eds., NEGOTIATING SECURITY: AN ARMS CONTROL READER (Washington, D.C.: The Carnegie Endowment for International Peace, 1979), pp. 160-61.
5   Reagan, p. 2.
6   *Reagan Alters Policy on A-Fuel Recycling,* THE WASHINGTON POST, 9 June 1980, p. A3.
7   Peter A. Bradford, *The Man/Machine Interface,* Speech before the Public Citizen Forum, Washington D.C., March 8, 1982.
8   *White House Text of President Reagan's Oct. 8 Policy Statement on Nuclear Power,* CONGRESSIONAL QUARTERLY WEEKLY REPORT 39, no. 42 (October 17, 1981): 2034.

CHAPTER ELEVEN

1   Spurgeon M. Keeny and Wolfgang K.H. Panofsky, *MAD Versus NUTS: Can Doctrine or Weaponry Remedy the Mutual Hostage Relationship of the Superpowers?* FOREIGN AFFAIRS 60, no. 2 (Winter 1981/1982): 289.
2   William H. Kincade, *American Interests in Strategic Arms Control: Past, Present and Future,* Paper presented to the Chicago Council on Foreign Relations, October 19, 1979, p. 12-13.

3   Herbert Scoville, Jr., MX: PRESCRIPTION FOR DISASTER (Cambridge, Mass.: The MIT Press, 1981), p. 79-80.
4   Thomas P. O'Neil, Jr., speech before Merrimac College graduation, North Andover, Massachusetts, May 23, 1982.

CHAPTER TWELVE

1   Amory B. Lovins, et al., *Nuclear Power and Nuclear Bombs,* FOREIGN AFFAIRS 58 (Summer 1980): 1148.
2   Ibid., p. 1172.
3   Ibid., p. 1149-73.
4   Clarence D. Long, *Nuclear Proliferation: Can Congress Act in Time?* INTERNATIONAL SECURITY 4 (Spring 1977): 52-79.
5   *Text of President's News Conference,* THE NEW YORK TIMES, 1 April 1982, p. 22.
6   Paul C. Warnke, *We Should Heed the Call for Nuclear Arms Freeze,* THE CHICAGO SUN-TIMES, 3 April 1982, p. 20.
7   Robert Stobaugh and Daniel Yergin, eds., ENERGY FUTURE, Report of the Energy Project at the Harvard Business School (New York: Random House, 1979), p. 142.
8   Congressional Research Service, NUCLEAR PROLIFERATION FACTBOOK (Washington, D.C.: Government Printing Office, 1980): 13.

Selected Bibliography

ABC News Closeup: Near Armageddon: The Spread of Nuclear Weapons in the Middle East. New York: American Broadcasting Companies Inc., 27 April 1981.

Altering of U.S. Nonproliferation Policy Pushed by Reagan Transition Group. NUCLE-ONICS WEEK, 18 December 1980, pp. 2–3.

Angry Kemeny Commission Promises to Recommend Major Changes At NRC. INSIDE NRC (August 24, 1979): 1.

Anti-Nukes, U.S. Style. NEWSWEEK, 23 November, 1981, pp. 44--49.

Auerbach, Stuart. *India Proposing Amicable End to Nuclear Contract.* THE WASHING-TON POST, 4 February 1981, p. A1, A14.

Baker, Steven J., *Arms Transfers and Nuclear Proliferation.* In William H. Kincade and Jeffrey D. Poro, eds., NEGOTIATING SECURITY: AN ARMS CONTROL READER, pp. 160, 161. Washington, D.C.: The Carnegie Endowment for International Peace, 1979.

Ball, Desmond. *Counterforce Targeting: How New? How Viable?* ARMS CONTROL TODAY 11, no. 2 (February 1981): 1–9.

Ball, George W. Testimony before Public Forum on the Nuclear Weapons Freeze and Reductions Resolution. Washington, D.C., March 22, 1982.

Betts, Richard K. *Nuclear Proliferation after Osirak.* ARMS CONTROL TODAY 11, no. 7 (September 1981): 1–8.

Bindon, George and Sitoo Makerji. *How Canada's and India's Nuclear Roles have been Sadly Misrepresented.* SCIENCE FORUM 10 (February 1977): 3–7.

Blechman, Barry M. *The Comprehensive Test Ban Negotiations: Can They be Revitalized?* ARMS CONTROL TODAY 11, no. 5 (June 1981): 1–8.

Bradford, Peter A. Testimony before the Subcommittee on International Security and Scientific Affairs and the Subcommittee on International Economic Policy and Trade, Committee on Foreign Affairs, U.S. House of Representatives. Washington, D.C., March 18, 1982.

Bradford, Peter A. *The Man/Machine Interface.* Speech before the Public Citizen Forum: Washington, D.C. March 8, 1982.

Bray, Frank T. J. and Michael L. Moodie. *Nuclear Politics in India.* SURVIVAL 20 (May–June 1977): 111–16.

Bundy, McGeorge. *Ship Fuel to India.* Editorial. THE WASHINGTON POST, 13 June 1980, p. A19.

Burnham, David. *Freeze On Building Of Nuclear Plants Rejected By House.* THE NEW YORK TIMES, 30 November 1979, p. 1.

Burt, Richard. *U.S. Reported Reviewing Sale of Nuclear Fuel to India.* THE NEW YORK TIMES, 4 June 1980, p. A3.

Calder, Nigel. NUCLEAR NIGHTMARES: AN INVESTIGATION INTO POSSIBLE WARS. New York: Viking Press, 1980.

Campaign For Safe Energy. *Missing Links in the Chain Reaction: A Summary of the Presidential Candidates' Positions on Nuclear Power.* Boston, 30 May 1980. (Mimeo.)

Carter, Jimmy. NUCLEAR POWER POLICY, APRIL 7, 1977. Presidential Documents. April 18, 1977. vol. 13, no. 15.

Carter, Luther J. *Relaxation Seen in Nonproliferation Policy.* SCIENCE, 5 October 1979, pp. 32–36.

CBS Evening News. Transcript of CBS Evening News. New York: CBS, Inc., 19 June 1980.

CBS Evening News. Transcript of CBS Evening News. New York: CBS, Inc., 5 March 1981.

CBS Evening News. Transcript of CBS Evening News. New York: CBS, Inc., 6 March 1981.

CHALLENGES FOR U.S. NATIONAL SECURITY: DEFENSE SPENDING AND THE ECONOMY, THE STRATEGIC BALANCE AND STRATEGIC ARMS LIMITATIONS. Washington, D.C.: The Carnegie Endowment for International Peace, 1981.

Chapman, William. *Japan Plans to Request Removal of U.S. Nuclear Fuel Restrictions.* THE WASHINGTON POST, 12 February 1981, p. A36.

Christensen, John. *Dropping a Bomb: The Not-So-Secret Secret.* STAR-BULLETIN (Honolulu), 5 December 1979, p. E1.

Clausen, Peter. *Nuclear Supply Policies After Osirak.* ARMS CONTROL TODAY 11, no. 7 (September 1981): 3–4.

Clear Signals on Nuclear Fuel. Editorial. THE WASHINGTON POST, 22 September 1980, p. A14.

Collins, Larry. *Combating Nuclear Terrorism.* THE NEW YORK TIMES MAGAZINE, 14 December 1980, pp. 37–39, 158–164.

CONGRESSIONAL RECORD, 29 November 1979, p. 11340–61.

CONGRESSIONAL RECORD, 18 September 1980, p. 9078.

CONGRESSIONAL RECORD, 23 September 1980, p. 13208.

CONGRESSIONAL RECORD, 24 September 1980, p. 13249.

CONGRESSIONAL RECORD, 17 March 1981, p. 2237.

Congressional Research Service. ISRAELI RAID INTO IRAQ. Issue Brief No. IB81103. Washington, D.C.: Government Printing Office, October 1, 1981.

Congressional Research Service. NUCLEAR ENERGY: ENRICHMENT AS REPROCESSING OF NUCLEAR FUELS. Issue Brief No. IB77126. Washington, D.C.: Government Printing Office, January 20, 1982.

Congressional Research Service. NUCLEAR ENERGY POLICY. Issue Brief No. IB78005. Washington, D.C.: Government Printing Office, July 27, 1981.

Congressional Research Service. NUCLEAR ENERGY: PROTECTION OF INTERNATIONAL NUCLEAR SHIPMENTS. Issue Brief No. IB1121. Washington, D.C.: Government Printing Office, January 8, 1982.

Congressional Research Service. NUCLEAR PROLIFERATION FACTBOOK. Washington, D.C.: Government Printing Office, 1977.

Congressional Research Service. NUCLEAR PROLIFERATION FACTBOOK. Washington, D.C.: Government Printing Office, 1980.

Congressional Research Service. NUCLEAR WEAPONS: PRODUCTION FROM COMMERCIAL PLUTONIUM. Issue Brief No. IB1168. Washington, D.C.: Government Printing Office, January 8, 1982.

Congressional Research Service. NUCLEAR WEAPONS PROLIFERATION: LEGISLATION FOR POLICY AND OTHER MEASURES. Issue Brief No. IB77011. Washington, D.C.: Government Printing Office, November 14, 1978.

Congressional Research Service. NUCLEAR WEAPONS: U.S. NONPROLIFERATION POLICY IN THE 97TH CONGRESS (1981–82). Issue Brief No. IB81014. Washington, D.C.: Government Printing Office, September 14, 1981.

Congressional Research Service. READER ON NUCLEAR PROLIFERATION. Washington, D.C.: Government Printing Office, 1978.

Congressional Research Service. READER ON NUCLEAR PROLIFERATION. Washington, D.C.: Government Printing Office, 1980.

Congressional Research Service. U.S./SOVIET MILITARY BALANCE: STATISTICAL TRENDS, 1970–1980. Report No. 81-233 S. Washington, D.C.: Government Printing Office, October 1981.

Cook, Don. *How Carter's Nuclear Policy Backfired Abroad.* FORTUNE 98 (October 23, 1978): 124–36.

Democratic National Committee. OFFICIAL REPORT OF THE PROCEEDINGS OF THE DEMOCRATIC NATIONAL CONVENTION. Washington, D.C.: Democratic National Committee, 1980.

DOE, AIF See Different Nuclear Power Futures. ENERGY DAILY, 23 January 1981, p. 3.

Don't Reload Tarapur. THE NEW YORK TIMES, 9 September 1980, p. 18.

Downey, Thomas J. *Against Trident II.* THE NEW YORK TIMES, February 11, 1982, p. A35.

Downie, Leonard, Jr. *Swiss Send Nuclear Aid to Pakistan.* THE WASHINGTON POST, 21 September 1980, p. A1, 22.

Dunn, Lewis A. *Half Past India's Bang.* FOREIGN POLICY 36 (Fall 1979): 71–105.

Editorial Research Reports. U.S. FOREIGN POLICY: FUTURE DIRECTIONS. Washington, D.C.: Congressional Quarterly, Inc., 1979.

The Energy Defense Project. DISPERSED, DECENTRALIZED AND RENEWABLE ENERGY SOURCES: ALTERNATIVES TO NATIONAL VULNERABILITY AND WAR. Washington, D.C.: Federal Energy Management Agency, 1980.

Fallows, James. NATIONAL DEFENSE. New York: Random House, 1981.

Faltermayer, Edmund. *Keeping the Peaceful Atom from Raising the Risk of War.* FORTUNE, 9 April 1979, pp. 90–96.

Feiveson, Harold A. and T.B. Taylor. *Security Implications of Alternative Fission Futures.*

BULLETIN OF ATOMIC SCIENTISTS, December 1976, 14–18, 46, 48.

Fialka, John J. *Why the AEC Failed to Tell of Lost Nuclear Material.* THE WASHINGTON STAR, 23 March 1978, p. A4.

Fuel to India. Transcript of the MacNeil/Lehrer Report. New York: Educational Broadcasting Corporation, 16 September 1980.

GAO, Reagan Transition Team Differ on Where to Put Export Office. NUCLEONICS WEEK, 12 February 1981, p. 6.

GAO Suggests Amendments to NNPA in Draft of Report to Congress. NUCLEONICS WEEK, 12 February 1981, p. 5.

General Accounting Office. Comptroller General. REPORT TO THE CONGRESS: ADMINISTRATION OF U.S. LICENSING SHOULD BE CONSOLIDATED TO BE MORE RESPONSIVE TO INDUSTRY. Washington, D.C.: Government Printing Office, 31 October 1978.

General Accounting Office. Comptroller General. REPORT TO THE CONGRESS: ASSESSMENT OF U.S. AND INTERNATIONAL CONTROLS OVER THE PEACEFUL USES OF NUCLEAR ENERGY. Washington, D.C.: Government Printing Office, 14 September 1976.

General Accounting Office. Comptroller General. REPORT TO·THE CONGRESS: EVALUATION OF SELECTED FEATURES OF U.S. NUCLEAR NONPROLIFERATION LAW AND POLICY. Washington, D.C.: Government Printing Office, 18 December 1980.

General Accounting Office. Comptroller General. REPORT TO THE CONGRESS: EVALUATION OF U.S. EFFORTS TO PROMOTE NUCLEAR NONPROLIFERATION TREATY. Washington, D.C.: Government Printing Office, 31 July 1980.

General Accounting Office. Comptroller General. REPORT TO THE CONGRESS: NUCLEAR FUEL REPROCESSING AND THE PROBLEMS OF SAFEGUARDING AGAINST THE SPREAD OF NUCLEAR WEAPONS. Washington, D.C.: Government Printing Office, 18 March 1980.

General Accounting Office. Comptroller General. REPORT TO THE CONGRESS: THE NUCLEAR NONPROLIFERATION ACT OF 1978 SHOULD BE SELECTIVELY MODIFIED. Washington, D.C.: Government Printing Office, 21 May 1981.

General Accounting Office. Comptroller General. REPORT TO THE CONGRESS: U.S. ENERGY ASSISTANCE TO DEVELOPING COUNTRIES: CLARIFICATION AND COORDINATION NEEDED. Washington, D.C.: Government Printing Office, 28 March 1980.

General Accounting Office. Comptroller General. REPORT TO THE CONGRESS: U.S. NUCLEAR NONPROLIFERATION POLICY: IMPACT ON EXPORTS AND NUCLEAR INDUSTRY COULD NOT BE DETERMINED. Washington, D.C.: Government Printing Office, 23 September 1980.

Gilinsky, Victor. Speech before the League of Women Voters Education Fund. Silver Spring, Maryland. November 17, 1980.

Gilinsky, Victor. Testimony before the Committee on Foreign Relations, U.S. Senate, Washington, D.C., December 2, 1981.

Glenn, John H., Jr. *No Fuel for Tarapur.* THE WASHINGTON POST, 22 September 1980, p. A15.

Goheen, Robert F. *Nuclear Fuel to India: Buying Time.* Editorial. THE WASHINGTON POST, 27 June 1980, p. A10.

Graham, Bradley. *Bonn's Orderly Rule is Ruffled by Opponents of Nuclear Power.* THE WASHINGTON POST, 15 February 1981, pp. A1, 26.

Graham, Bradley and Leonard Downie, Jr. *Europe's Antinuclear Movement Worries NATO Defense Officials.* THE WASHINGTON POST, 29 March 1981, p. A20.

Gray, Colin S. *Wanted: An Arms Control Policy.* ARMS CONTROL TODAY 12, no. 2 (February 1982): 1–9.

The Guardian. WINDSCALE: A SUMMARY OF THE EVIDENCE AND THE ARGUMENTS. London: The Guardian Newspapers Limited, 1977.

Gwertzman, Bernard. *U.S. Monitors Signs of Atom Explosion Near South Africa.* THE NEW YORK TIMES, 26 October 1979, p. 1.

Hart, Gary. Testimony before the Subcommittee on International Economic Policy and Trade, Committee on Foreign Affairs, U.S. House of Representatives, Washington, D.C., March 3, 1982.

Hennies, H.H.; P. Jansen; and G. Kessler. *A West German Perspective on the Need for the Plutonium-fueled LMFBR.* NUCLEAR NEWS, June 1979, pp. 69–75.

Herbers, John. *Nuclear Energy Emerging as a Key Issue in Campaigning for Presidency.* THE NEW YORK TIMES, 21 February 1980, p. B10.

Hershey, Robert D., Jr. *Can Reagan Lift the Cloud Over Nuclear Power?* THE NEW YORK TIMES, 8 March 1981, pp. F1, 22.

Hussein, Saddam. Statement during Cabinet Meeting June 23, 1981. Foreign Broadcast Service-MEA-81-121, June 24, 1981.

IAEA SAFEGUARDS: AN INTRODUCTION. Vienna: International Atomic Energy Agency, 1981.

India Reacts Calmly to Setback in U.S. on Atom Fuel. THE NEW YORK TIMES, 12 September 1980, p. A10.

Jaroslavsky, Rich. *Bid to Boost U.S. Nuclear Power Funding Sparks Quiet Energy Agency-OMB Fight.* THE WALL STREET JOURNAL, 25 February 1981, p. 17.

Johnson, Brian. WHOSE POWER TO CHOOSE? INTERNATIONAL INSTITUTIONS AND THE CONFLICT OF NUCLEAR ENERGY. London: International Institute for Environment and Development, 1977.

Katz, Arthur M. LIFE AFTER NUCLEAR WAR. Cambridge, Mass.: Ballinger Publishing Co., 1982.

Keeny, Spurgeon M., Jr. et al. NUCLEAR POWER ISSUES AND CHOICES, Report of the Nuclear Energy and Policy Study Group. Cambridge, Mass.: Ballinger Publishing Co., 1977.

Keeny, Spurgeon M. and Wolfgang K.H. Panofsky. *MAD Versus NUTS: Can Doctrine or Weaponry Remedy the Mutual Hostage Relationship of the Superpowers?* FOREIGN AFFAIRS 60, no. 2 (Winter 1981/1982): 287–304.

Kincade, William H. *American Interests in Strategic Arms Control: Past, Present and Future.* Paper presented to the Chicago Council on Foreign Relations, October 19, 1979.

Kincade, William H. *Missile Vulnerability Reconsidered.* ARMS CONTROL TODAY 11, no. 5 (May 1981): 1–8.

Kincade, William H. and Jeffrey D. Poro, eds. NEGOTIATING SECURITY: AN ARMS CONTROL READER. Washington, D.C.: The Carnegie Endowment for International Peace, 1979.

Krepon, Michael. *Reagan's Approach: START OFF From the Beginning.* ARMS CONTROL TODAY 11, no. 8 (October 1981): 1–7.

Lanouette, William J. *Under Scrutiny by a Divided Government, the Nuclear Industry Tries to Unite.* NATIONAL JOURNAL 2 (12 January 1980): 44–48.

Lanouette, William J. *U.S. Nuclear Industry Can't Expect Much Help From Abroad.* NATIONAL JOURNAL 29 (21 July 1979): 1207–10.

LDC NUCLEAR POWER PROSPECTS, 1975–1990: COMMERCIAL, ECONOMIC AND SECURITY IMPLICATIONS. Washington, D.C.: Energy Research and Development Administration, 1976.

Leventhal, Paul. Testimony before the Subcommittee on International Economic Policy and Trade, Committee on Foreign Affairs, U.S. House of Representatives, Washington, D.C., March 3, 1982.

Lindsey, Robert. *Reagan Says America Should Not Bar Others From A-Bomb Output.* THE NEW YORK TIMES, 1 February 1980, p. A12.

Long, Clarence D. *Nuclear Proliferation: Can Congress Act in Time?* INTERNATIONAL SECURITY 4 (Spring 1977): 52–79.

Lovins, Amory B. *Nuclear Reactors and Power-reactor Plutonium.* NATURE 283 (28 February 1980): 817–23.

Lovins, Amory B. and L. Hunter Lovins. ENERGY/WAR: BREAKING THE NUCLEAR LINK. San Francisco: Friends of the Earth, 1980.

Lovins, Amory B.; L. Hunter Lovins; and Leonard Ross. *Nuclear Power and Nuclear Bombs.* FOREIGN AFFAIRS 58 (Summer 1980): 1137–77.

Markey, Edward J. *A Tougher Stand—Starting with India.* Editorial. THE WASHINGTON POST, 9 June 1980, p. A21.

Markey, Edward J. *Dear Colleague* to other members of Congress, May 22, 1980.

Markey, Edward J., *Dear Colleague* to other members of Congress, September 18, 1980.

Markey, Edward J. Letter to the President, May 22, 1980.

Marwah, Onkar. *India's Nuclear and Space Programs: Intent and Policy.* INTERNATIONAL SECURITY 2 (Fall 1977): 96–121.

McCormack, Mike. *Dear Colleague* to other members of Congress, July 14, 1980.

McGraw, Marsha M. *The NPT Review Conference.* ARMS CONTROL TODAY 11. no. 2 (February 1981): 3-9.

THE MILITARY BALANCE 1981-1982. London: The International Institute for Strategic Studies, 1981.

Miller, G. Wayne. *Could Someone Blow Up Boston?* THE BOSTON GLOBE, 10 September 1978, pp. 10-11, 16-18..

Miller, Judith. *Senate Opens Debate on Uranium Sale to India: Vote Seen as a Policy Test.* THE NEW YORK TIMES, 24 September 1980, p. 6.

Morland, Howard. *The H-Bomb Secret: To Know is to Ask Why.* THE PROGRESSIVE, November 1979, pp. 14-23.

New Jersey Journal. THE NEW YORK TIMES, 5 October 1980, sec. 11, p. 3.

A New Outcry Over Nukes. NEWSWEEK, 29 March 1982, pp. 18-20.

THE NEW YORK TIMES, 5 October 1980, Sec. 11, p. 3.

1980: Bittersweet Times for Uranium. ENERGY DAILY, 18 March 1981, p. 2.

1980 Republican Platform Text. CONGRESSIONAL QUARTERLY WEEKLY REPORT 38, no. 29, (19 July 1980): 2052.

The Nuclear Arms Race. NEWSWEEK, 5 October 1981, pp. 32-39.

Nuclear Cave. Editorial. THE WALL STREET JOURNAL, 9 March 1980, p. 18.

NUCLEAR ENERGY: DARK OUTLOOK. Washington, D.C.: Washington Analysis Corporation, December 1979.

Nuclear Hypocrisy. Editorial. THE WALL STREET JOURNAL, 24 September 1980, p. 30.

Nuclear Nearsightedness. Editorial. THE WASHINGTON POST, 9 May 1980, p. A22.

The Nuclear Nonproliferation Act of 1978. INTERNATIONAL SECURITY 3 (Fall 1978): 44-46.

Nuclear Reactors and Nuclear Bombs. Speech by Victor Gilinsky, Commissioner, U.S. Nuclear Regulatory Commission, Silver Spring, Maryland, November 17, 1980.

Nuclear Regulatory Commission, *Transcript of Proceedings*, Washington, D.C., 16 July 1979, p. 48.

NUCLEONICS WEEK 21, no. 51 (December 18, 1980): 1.

Oberdorfer, Don. U.S. Is Ending 18-Year Nuclear Pact With India. THE WASHINGTON POST, 23 April 1981, p. A19.

Omang, Joanne. *Panel Votes 6-Month Ban on New A-Plants.* THE WASHINGTON POST, 10 May 1979, p. A13.

Office of Technology Assessment. NUCLEAR PROLIFERATION AND SAFEGUARDS. New York: Praeger, 1977.

Organization for Economic Co-operation and Development. Nuclear Energy Agency. SUMMARY OF NUCLEAR POWER AND FUEL CYCLE DATA IN OECD MEMBER COUNTRIES. Organization for Economic Co-operation and Development, March 1981.

O'Toole, Thomas. *NRC against U.S. uranium flow to India.* Washington Post/Los Angeles Times News Service. THE BOSTON GLOBE, 17 May 1980, p. 3.

Pakistan Hoodwinks World Over H-Bomb. THE ATLANTA CONSTITUTION, 2 July 1979, p. 1.

Paladino, Nunzio. Chairman, Nuclear Regulatory Commission, Letter to Senator Alan Simpson, Chairman Subcommittee on Nuclear Regulation, Committee on Environment and Public Works, U.S. Senate, November 27, 1981.

Perlmutter, Sandra P. and Elizabeth C. Burke, eds. OFFICIAL REPORT OF THE PROCEEDINGS OF THE DEMOCRATIC NATIONAL CONVENTION. Washington, D.C.: Democratic National Committee, 1980.

Plattner, Andy. *Reagan Nuclear Policy Draws Mixed Reaction in Congress.* CONGRESSIONAL QUARTERLY WEEKLY REPORT 39, no. 42 (17 October 1981): 2033-34.

Pollock, Richard. *The Islamic Bomb.* CRITICAL MASS JOURNAL, July 1980, pp. 4-5, 15.

Power, Paul F. *The Reagan Nonproliferation Policy.* ARMS CONTROL TODAY 11, no. 8 (October 1981): 6-8.

The Public Interest Groups Fight Back. DUN'S REVIEW, January 1981, pp. 56-57.

Randall, Nan. *Envisioning How We Might Suffer in Two Kinds of Nuclear Attacks.* THE WASHINGTON POST, 29 January 1978, pp. C1, 4-6.

Reagan, Ronald. Statement by the President, Press Release, Office of the Press Secretary, The White House, July 16, 1981.

Reagan's Arms Buildup. NEWSWEEK, 8 June 1981, pp. 28-48.

Reilly, Ann M. *The Big Battles Over Energy.* DUN'S REVIEW, January 1981, pp. 48-49, 54-55, 60.

Richardson, Michael. *Hanoi's Nuclear Hand-Me-Down.* FAR EASTERN ECONOMIC REVIEW, 26 May 1978, pp. 8-9.

Richter, Roger. Testimony before the Committee on Foreign Relations, U.S. Senate, Washington, D.C., June 19, 1981.

Rosenbaum, David M. *Nuclear Terror.* INTERNATIONAL SECURITY 1 (Winter 1977): 140-61.

Rosenbaum, Walter A. ENERGY, POLITICS AND PUBLIC POLICY. Washington, D.C.: Congressional Quarterly Press, 1981.

Ross, Leonard. *How 'Atoms for Peace' Became Bombs for Sale.* THE NEW YORK TIMES MAGAZINE, 5 December 1976, pp. 39-123.

Schechter, Bruce. *Could Iraq Have Built the Bomb?* DISCOVER (August 1981): 59-62.

Schell, Jonathan. *Reflections: The Fate of the Earth, Part I.* THE NEW YORKER (February 1, 1982): 47.

Scherr, Jacob and Thomas Stoel. *Atoms for Peace? Controlling the Spread of Nuclear Weapons.* AMICUS (Summer 1979): 18-35.

Scoville, Herbert Jr. *The MX and Minuteman Vulnerability.* Testimony before the Defense and Military Construction Subcommittee, Committee on Appropriations, U.S. Senate, May 7, 1980.

Scoville, Herbert, Jr. MX:PRESCRIPTION FOR DISASTER (Cambridge, Mass.: The MIT Press, 1981).

Sebramian, R. R. *India's Nuclear Situation: Where To?* INSTITUTE FOR DEFENSE STUDIES AND ANALYSES JOURNAL 10 (April-June 1978): 304-21.

Sell Nuclear Fuel to India? Interview with Representatives Mike McCormack and Jonathan B. Bingham. U.S. NEWS AND WORLD REPORT 18 August 1980 pp. 47-48.

Sethna, Dr. H.N. *India's Atomic Energy Programme—Past and Future.* INTERNATIONAL ATOMIC ENERGY AGENCY BULLETIN 21 (October 1979): 2-11.

Sheils, Merrill. *Reagan's Nuclear Reaction.* NEWSWEEK, 12 January 1981, pp. 62-64.

Singer, Michael and David Weir. *Nuclear Nightmare.* NEW WEST, 3 December 1979, pp. 15-34.

Sivard, Ruth Leger. WORLD MILITARY AND SOCIAL EXPENDITURES. Leesburg, Virginia: World Priorities, 1981.

Smith, Gerard C. THE REAGAN STRATEGIC PROGRAM. Washington, D.C.: The Arms Control Association, 1981.

Stares, Paul. *Outer Space: Arms or Arms Control.* ARMS CONTROL TODAY 11 no. 6 (July/August 1981): 1–8.

Stobaugh, Robert and Daniel Yergin, eds. ENERGY FUTURE, REPORT OF THE ENERGY PROJECT AT THE HARVARD BUSINESS SCHOOL. New York: Random House, 1979.

Sweet, William. *Nonproliferation Treaty and the Third World.* ALTERNATIVES 2 (December 1976): 405–20.

Tammen, Ronald L. *The Reagan Strategic Program.* ARMS CONTROL TODAY 11, no. 11 (December 1981): 1–6.

Text of President's News Conference. THE NEW YORK TIMES, 1 April 1982, p. 22.

This Nuclear Decision is Contagious. THE NEW YORK TIMES, 12 May 1980, p. A18.

Tolchin, Martin. *Atom Fuel for India: A 38-Ton Controversy.* THE NEW YORK TIMES, 26 September 1980, p. 3.

Tsuchiya, Haruki. *Soft Energy Planning for Japan.* SOFT ENERGY NOTES, February/March 1981, pp. 8–9.

Tyler, Patrick E. *Reagan Rejects Bailout Plan for Idle Nuclear Plant.* THE WASHINGTON POST, 12 April 1981, p. A10.

United Press International. *Carter's Policy on Reprocessing A-Fuel Scrapped.* THE WASHINGTON POST, 14 March 1981, p. A12.

U.S. Congress. House. Committee on Foreign Affairs. HEARINGS AND MARKUP ON H. CON. RES. 367 AND 368, RESOLUTIONS OF DISAPPROVAL PERTAINING TO THE SHIPMENT OF NUCLEAR FUEL TO INDIA. 96th Congress, 2nd Session, Washington, D.C.: Government Printing Office, 1980.

U.S. Congress. House. Subcommittee on Energy and the Environment of the Committee on Interior and Insular Affairs. UNITED STATES NUCLEAR NONPROLIFERATION POLICY. 96th Congress, 2nd Session, Washington, D.C.: Government Printing Office, 1980.

U.S. Congress. House. Subcommittee on Oversight and Investigations, Committee on Interior and Insular Affairs. HEARING ON THE PROPOSALS TO OBTAIN PLUTONIUM FROM COMMERCIAL SPENT FUEL FROM U.S. REACTORS. 97th Congress, 1st Session, Washington, D.C.: Government Printing Office, 1981.

U.S. Congress. House. Subcommittee on Oversight and Investigations, Committee on Interior and Insular Affairs. HEARING ON NUCLEAR FUEL CYCLE POLICY AND THE FUTURE OF NUCLEAR POWER. 97th Congress, 1st Session, Washington, D.C.: Government Printing Office, 1981.

U.S. Congress. House. Subcommittee on Oversight and Investigations of the Committee on Interstate and Foreign Commerce. POTENTIAL DISPLACEMENT OF OIL BY NUCLEAR ENERGY AND COAL IN ELECTRIC UTILITIES. 96th Congress, 2nd Session, Washington, D.C.: Government Printing Office, 1980.

U.S. Congress. Joint Committee on Atomic Energy. ATOMIC POWER AND PRIVATE ENTERPRISE. 82nd Congress, 2nd Session, Washington, D.C.: Government Printing Office, 1952.

U.S. Congress. Senate. Committee on Foreign Relations. OFFICIAL TRANSCRIPT: PROPOSED NUCLEAR FUEL SHIPMENT TO INDIA (TARAPUR) AND THE VOTE ON DISAPPROVING THE SHIPMENT. Washington, D.C.: Anderson Reporting, 10 September 1980.

U.S. Congress. Senate. Committee on Foreign Relations. PENDING NUCLEAR ISSUES BETWEEN THE UNITED STATES, INDIA AND PAKISTAN. 96th Congress, 2nd Session, Washington, D.C.: Government Printing Office, 1980.

U.S. Congress. Senate. Committee on Foreign Relations. TARAPUR NUCLEAR FUEL EXPORT, Report of the Committee on Foreign Relations, United States Senate together with Minority Views. 96th Congress, 2nd Session, Washington, D.C.: Government Printing Office, 1980.

U.S. Congress. Senate. Committee on Foreign Relations and Committee on Governmental Affairs. JOINT HEARINGS ON THE ISSUE OF WHETHER TO SHIP NUCLEAR FUEL TO INDIA FOR THE TARAPUR POWER REACTORS. 96th Congress, 2nd Session, Washington, D.C.: Government Printing Office, 1980.

U.S. Congress. Senate. Subcommittee on Energy, Nuclear Proliferation and Federal Services of the Committee on Governmental Affairs. ERRONEOUS DECLASSIFICATION OF NUCLEAR WEAPONS INFORMATION, PART I. 96th Congress, 1st Session, Washington, D.C.: Government Printing Office, 1979.

U.S. Congress. Senate. Subcommittee on Energy, Nuclear Proliferation and Federal Services of the Committee on Governmental Affairs. ERRONEOUS DECLASSIFICATION OF NUCLEAR WEAPONS INFORMATION, PART II. 96th Congress, 1st Session, Washington, D.C.: Government Printing Office, 1979.

U.S. Department of Energy. Energy Information Administration. NUCLEAR POWER FORECASTS FOR THE DEVELOPING COUNTRIES THROUGH THE YEAR 2000. Washington, D.C.: Department of Energy, 1980.

U.S. Department of Energy. Energy Information Administration. Office of Applied Analysis. Nuclear Energy Analysis Division. CHRONOLOGY OF NUCLEAR POWER FORECASTS FOR THE U.S. AND THE WORLD OUTSIDE CENTRALLY PLANNED ECONOMIC AREAS. Washington, D.C.: Department of Energy, October 1980.

U.S. Department of Energy. International Affairs Office of Market Analysis. INTERNATIONAL ENERGY INDICATORS. Washington, D.C.: Department of Energy, January 1981.

Unreliable Customer. Editorial. THE WASHINGTON POST, 12 September 1980, p. A18.

Van Doren, Charles N. *Iraq, Israel and the Middle East Proliferation Problem.* Report prepared for the Arms Control Association, June 25, 1981.

Walske, Carl. *Nuclear Electric Power and the Proliferation of Nuclear Weapons.* INTERNATIONAL SECURITY 1, no. 3 (Winter 1977): 106.

Warnke, Paul C. *Nuclear Weapons Escalation Versus Arms Control.* Testimony before Congressional Ad Hoc Hearing on the Full Implications of the Military Budget, March 18, 1982.

Warnke, Paul C. *We Should Heed the Call for Nuclear Arms Freeze.* THE CHICAGO TRIBUNE, 3 April 1982, p. 20.

Washington Analysis Corporation, A subsidiary of Bache, Halsey, Stuart, Shields Incorporated. *Nuclear Energy: Dark Outlook* (Washington, D.C., December 21, 1979). (Mimeo.).

Weaver, Kenneth F. *Our Energy Predicament.* NATIONAL GEOGRAPHIC, February 1981, pp. 2–114.

Wechsler, Jill. *Powerful Support for Industry. DUN'S REVIEW,* January 1981, p. 61.

Weisskopf, Victor A. *On Avoiding Nuclear Holocaust.* TECHNOLOGY REVIEW, no. 1 (October 1980), pp. 28–35.

Weissman, Steve and Herbert Krosney. THE ISLAMIC BOMB. New York: Times Books, 1981.

White House Text of President Reagan's Oct. 8 Policy Statement on Nuclear Power. CONGRESSIONAL QUARTERLY WEEKLY REPORT 39, no. 42 (October 17, 1981): 2034.

Willis, David K. *On the Trail of the A-Bomb Makers.* THE CHRISTIAN SCIENCE MONITOR. November 30–December 4, 1981.

Wit, Joel. *'Sanctuaries' and Security: Suggestions for ASW Arms Control.* ARMS CONTROL TODAY 10, no. 9 (October 1980): 1–7.

Wohlstetter, Albert. *Spreading the Bomb Without Quite Breaking the Rules.* FOREIGN AFFAIRS 25 (Winter 1976–1977): 88–96, 145–79.

Wohlstetter, Albert; Thomas A. Brown; Gregory S. Jones; David McGarvey; Henry Rowen: Vince Taylor; and Roberta Wohlstetter. SWORDS FROM PLOUGHSHARES: THE MILITARY POTENTIAL OF CIVILIAN NUCLEAR ENERGY. Chicago: University of Chicago Press, 1977.

Wohlstetter, Roberta. *Terror on a Grand Scale.* SURVIVAL, May–June 1976, pp. 98–104.

Wohlstetter, Roberta. *U.S. Peaceful Aid and the Indian Bomb.* In Albert Wohlstetter, Victor Gilinsky, Robert Gillette, Roberta Wohlstetter. NUCLEAR POLICIES: FUEL WITHOUT THE BOMB. Cambridge, Mass.: Ballinger Publishing Co. 1979.

World Bank. ENERGY IN THE DEVELOPING COUNTRIES. Washington, D.C.: World Bank, 1980.

Wydler, John W. *Dear Colleague* to other members of Congress, September 18, 1980.

Yergin, Daniel. *The Terrifying Prospect.* ATLANTIC, April 1977, pp. 46–65.

Zagoria, Donald S. *The Superpowers and the Arms Race. ARMS CONTROL TODAY* 10, no. 9 (October 1980): 3–10.

Index

About the Authors

Congressman Edward J. Markey, a Democrat, represents the Seventh District of Massachusetts. Elected to the House in 1976, Congressman Markey is chairman of the Interior and Insular Affairs Subcommittee on Oversight and Investigations and a member of the Subcommittee on Energy and the Environment. He is also a member of the Energy and Commerce Committee and the following subcommittees: Energy Conservation and Power; Fossil and Synthetic Fuels; and Telecommunications, Consumer Protection, and Finance.

Douglas C. Waller is a senior legislative assistant for arms control and nuclear proliferation on Congressman Markey's staff.